THE
GENTLEMEN'S
BOOK OF
ETIQUETTE
AND MANUAL OF
POLITENESS

Published by Hesperus Press Limited
28 Mortimer Street, London W1W 7RD
www.hesperuspress.com

The Gentlemen's Book of Etiquette first published in 1860
First published by Hesperus Press Limited, 2014

Typeset and designed by Madeline Meckiffe

ISBN: 978-1-84391-541-6

THE GENTLEMEN'S BOOK OF ETIQUETTE AND MANUAL OF POLITENESS

HESPERUS

CONTENTS

INTRODUCTION

M AN was not intended to live like a bear or a hermit, apart from others of his own nature, and, philosophy and reason will each agree with me, that man was born for sociability and finds his true delight in society. Society is a word capable of many meanings, and used here in each and all of them. Society, *par excellence*; the world at large; the little clique to which he is bound by early ties; the companionship of friends or relatives; even society *tête à tête* with one dear sympathising soul, are pleasant states for a man to be in.

Taking the word in its most extended view, it is the world; but in the light we wish to impress in our book it is the smaller world of the changing, pleasant intercourse of each city or town in which our reader may chance to abide.

This society, composed, as it is, of many varying natures and elements, where each individual must submit to merge his own identity into the universal whole, which makes the word and state, is divided and subdivided into various cliques, and has a pastime for every disposition, grave or gay; and with each division rises up a new set of forms and ceremonies to be observed if you wish to glide down the current of polite life, smoothly and pleasantly.

The young man who makes his first entrance into the world of society, should know how to choose his friends, and next how to conduct himself towards them. Experience is, of course, the best guide, but at first starting this must come second-hand, from an older friend, or from books.

A judicious friend is the best guide; but how is the young man to know whom to choose? When at home this friend is easily selected; but in this country, where each bird leaves the parent nest as soon as his wings will bear him safely up, there are but few who stay amongst the friends at home.

Next then comes the instruction from books. True a book will not fully supply the place either of experience or friendly advice, still it may be made useful, and, carefully written from the experience of heads grown grey in society, with only well-authenticated rules, it will be a guide not to be despised by the young aspirant for favour in polite and refined circles.

You go into society from mixed motives; partly for pleasure, recreation after the fatigues of your daily duties, and partly that you may become known. In a republican country where one man's opportunities for rising are as good as those of another, ambition will lead every rising man into society.

You may set it down as a rule, that as you treat the world, so the world will treat you. Carry into the circles of society a refined, polished manner, and an amiable desire to please, and it will meet you with smiling grace, and lead you forward pleasantly along the flowery paths; go, on the contrary, with a brusque, rude manner, startling all the silky softness before you with cut and thrust remarks, carrying only the hard realities of life in your hand, and you will find society armed to meet you, showing only sharp corners and thorny places for your blundering footsteps to stumble against.

You will find in every circle that etiquette holds some sway; her rule is despotic in some places, in others mild, and easily set aside. Your first lesson in society will be to study where she reigns supreme, in her crown and holding her sceptre, and where she only glides in with a gentle hint or so, and timidly steps out if rebuked; and let your conduct be governed by the result of your observations. You will soon become familiar with the signs, and tell on your first entrance into a room whether kid gloves and exquisite finish of manner will be appropriate, or whether it is 'hail, fellow, well met' with the inmates. Remember, however, 'once a gentleman always a gentleman', and be sure that you can so carry out the rule, that in your most careless, joyous moments, when freest from the restraints of etiquette, you can still be recognisable as a *gentleman* by every act, word, or look.

Avoid too great a restraint of manner. Stiffness is not politeness, and, while you observe every rule, you may appear to heed none. To make your politeness part of yourself, inseparable from every action, is the height of gentlemanly elegance and finish of manner.

CHAPTER I

Conversation

O NE of the first rules for a guide in polite conversation, is to avoid political or religious discussions in general society. Such discussions lead almost invariably to irritating differences of opinion, often to open quarrels, and a coolness of feeling which might have been avoided by dropping the distasteful subject as soon as marked differences of opinion arose. It is but one out of many that can discuss either political or religious differences, with candour and judgement, and yet so far control his language and temper as to avoid either giving or taking offence.

I N their place, in circles which have met for such discussions, in a *tête à tête* conversation, in a small party of gentlemen where each is ready courteously to listen to the others, politics may be discussed with perfect propriety, but in the drawing room, at the dinner-table, or in the society of ladies, these topics are best avoided.

I F you are drawn into such a discussion without intending to be so, be careful that your individual opinion does not lead you into language and actions unbecoming a gentleman. Listen courteously to those whose opinions do not agree with yours, and *keep your temper*. A man in a passion ceases to be a gentleman.

E VEN if convinced that your opponent is utterly wrong, yield gracefully, decline further discussion, or dextrously turn the conversation, but do not obstinately defend your own opinion until you become angry, or more excited than is becoming to a gentleman.

M ANY there are who, giving their opinion, not as an *opinion* but as a *law*, will defend their position by such phrases, as – 'Well, if *I* were president, or governor, I would,' etc. – and while by the warmth of their argument they prove that they are utterly unable to govern their own temper, they will endeavour to persuade you that they are perfectly competent to take charge of the government of the nation.

R ETAIN, if you will, a fixed political opinion, yet do not parade it upon all occasions, and, above all, do not endeavour to *force* others to agree with you. Listen calmly to their ideas upon the same subjects, and if you cannot agree, differ politely, and while your opponent may set you down as a bad politician, let him be obliged to admit that you are a *gentleman*.

———⋅⊷⊙⊶⋅———

W IT and vivacity are two highly important ingredients in the conversation of a man in polite society, yet a straining for effect, or forced wit, is in excessively bad taste. There is no one more insupportable in society than the everlasting talkers who scatter puns, witticisms, and jokes with so profuse a hand that they become as tiresome as a comic newspaper, and whose loud laugh at their own wit drowns other voices which might speak matter more interesting. The really witty man does not shower forth his wit so indiscriminately; his charm consists in wielding his powerful weapon delicately and easily, and making each highly polished witticism come in the right place and moment to be effectual. While real wit is a most delightful gift, and its use a most charming accomplishment, it is, like many other bright weapons, dangerous to use too often. You may wound where you meant only to amuse, and remarks which you mean only in for general applications, may be construed into personal affronts, so, if you have the gift, use it wisely, and not too freely.

———⋅⊷⊙⊶⋅———

T HE most important requisite for a good conversational power is education, and, by this is meant, not merely the matter you may store in your memory from observation or books, though this is of vast importance, but it also includes the developing of the mental powers, and, above all, the comprehension.

———⋅⊷⊙⊶⋅———

'I N the present day an acquaintance with art, even if you have no love for it, is a *sine qua non* of good society. Music and painting are subjects which will be discussed in every direction around you. It is only in bad society that people go to the opera, concerts, and art exhibitions merely because it is the fashion, or to say they have been there; and if you confessed to such a weakness in really good society, you would be justly voted a puppy. For this, too, some book knowledge is indispensable. You should at least know the names of the more celebrated artists, composers, architects, sculptors, and so forth, and should be able to approximate their several schools.'

'P RECISION and accuracy must begin in the very outset; and if we neglect them in grammar, we shall scarcely acquire them in expressing our thoughts. But since there is no society without interchange of thought, and since the best society is that in which the best thoughts are interchanged in the best and most comprehensible manner, it follows that a proper mode of expressing ourselves is indispensable in good society.'

'T HE art of expressing one's thoughts neatly and suitably is one which, in the neglect of rhetoric as a study, we must practise for ourselves. The commonest thought well put is more useful in a social point of view, than the most brilliant idea jumbled out. What is well expressed is easily seized, and therefore readily responded to; the most poetic fancy may be lost to the hearer, if the language which conveys it is obscure. Speech is the gift which distinguishes man from animals, and makes society possible. He has but a poor appreciation of his high privilege as a human being, who neglects to cultivate, "God's great gift of speech".'

———❧———

'As I am not writing for men of genius, but for ordinary beings, I am right to state that an indispensable part of education is a knowledge of the literature of the English language. But *how* to read, is, for society more important than *what* we read. The man who takes up nothing but a newspaper, but reads it to *think*, to deduct conclusions from its premises, and form a judgement on its opinions, is more fitted for society than he, who having all the current literature and devoting his whole time to its perusal, swallows it all without digestion. In fact, the mind must be treated like the body, and however great its appetite, it will soon fall into bad health if it gorges, but does not ruminate. At the same time an acquaintance with the best current literature is necessary to modern society, and it is not sufficient to have read a book without being able to pass a judgement upon it. Conversation on literature is impossible, when your respondent can only say, "Yes. I like the book, but I really don't know why."'

———❧———

'An acquaintance with old English literature is not perhaps indispensable, but it gives a man great advantage in all kinds of society, and in some he is at a constant loss without it. The same may be said of foreign literature, which in the present day is almost as much discussed as our own; but, on the other hand, an acquaintance with home and foreign politics, with current history, and subjects of passing interest, is absolutely necessary; and a person of sufficient intelligence to join in good society, cannot dispense with his daily newspaper, his literary journal, and the principal reviews and magazines. The cheapness of every kind of literature, the facilities of our well-stored circulating libraries, our public reading rooms, and numerous excellent lectures on every possible subject, leave no excuse to poor or rich for an ignorance of any of the topics discussed in intellectual society. You may forget your Latin, Greek, French, German, and Mathematics, but if you frequent good company, you will never be allowed to forget that you are a citizen of the world.'

A MAN of real intelligence and cultivated mind, is generally modest. He may feel when in everyday society, that in intellectual acquirements he is above those around him; but he will not seek to make his companions feel their inferiority, nor try to display this advantage over them. He will discuss with frank simplicity the topics started by others, and endeavour to avoid starting such as they will not feel inclined to discuss. All that he says will be marked by politeness and deference to the feelings and opinions of others.

LA Bruyere says, 'The great charm of conversation consists less in the display of one's own wit and intelligence, than in the power to draw forth the resources of others; he who leaves you after a long conversation, pleased with himself and the part he has taken in the discourse, will be your warmest admirer. Men do not care to admire you, they wish you to be pleased with them; they do not seek for instruction or even amusement from your discourse, but they do wish you to be made acquainted with their talents and powers of conversation; and the true man of genius will delicately make all who come in contact with him, feel the exquisite satisfaction of knowing that they have appeared to advantage.'

Having admitted the above to be an incontestable fact, you will also see that it is as great an accomplishment to listen with an air of interest and attention, as it is to speak well.

To be a good listener is as indispensable as to be a good talker, and it is in the character of listener that you can most readily detect the man who is accustomed to good society. Nothing is more embarrassing to anyone who is speaking, than to perceive signs of weariness or inattention in the person whom he addresses.

Never interrupt anyone who is speaking; it is quite as rude to officiously supply a name or date about which another hesitates, unless you are asked to do so. Another gross breach of etiquette, is to anticipate the point of a story which another person is reciting, or to take it from his lips to finish it in your own language. Some persons plead as an excuse for this breach of etiquette, that the reciter was spoiling a good story by a bad manner, but this does not mend the matter. It is surely rude to give a man to understand that you do not consider him capable of finishing an anecdote that he has commenced.

I T is ill-bred to put on an air of weariness during a long speech from another person, and quite as rude to look at a watch, read a letter, flirt the leaves of a book, or in any other action show that you are tired of the speaker or his subject.

I N a general conversation, never speak when another person is speaking, and never try by raising your own voice to drown that of another. Never assume an air of haughtiness, or speak in a dictatorial manner; let your conversation be always amiable and frank, free from every affectation.

P UT yourself on the same level as the person to whom you speak, and under penalty of being considered a pedantic idiot, refraining from explaining any expression or word that you may use.

N EVER, unless you are requested to do so, speak of your own business or profession in society; to confine your conversation entirely to the subject or pursuit which is your own speciality is low-bred and vulgar.

————◦⟨◦⟩◦————

Make the subject for conversation suit the company in which you are placed. Joyous, light conversation will be at times as much out of place, as a sermon would be at a dancing party. Let your conversation be grave or gay as suits the time or place.

————◦⟨◦⟩◦————

In a dispute, if you cannot reconcile the parties, withdraw from them. You will surely make one enemy, perhaps two, by taking either side, in an argument when the speakers have lost their temper.

————◦⟨◦⟩◦————

Never gesticulate in everyday conversation, unless you wish to be mistaken for a fifth-rate comedian.

————◦⟨◦⟩◦————

Never ask anyone who is conversing with you to repeat his words. Nothing is ruder than to say, 'Pardon me, will you repeat that sentence – I did not hear you at first,' and thus imply that your attention was wandering when he first spoke.

————◦⟨◦⟩◦————

Never, during a general conversation, endeavour to concentrate the attention wholly upon yourself. It is quite as rude to enter into conversation with one of a group, and endeavour to draw him out of the circle of general conversation to talk with you alone.

———◦◦◦———

S PEAK of yourself but little. Your friends will find out your virtues without forcing you to tell them, and you may feel confident that it is equally unnecessary to expose your faults yourself.

———◦◦◦———

I N speaking of your friends, do not compare them, one with another. Speak of the merits of each one, but do not try to heighten the virtues of one by contrasting them with the vices of another.

———◦◦◦———

N O matter how absurd are the anecdotes that may be told in your presence, you must never give any sign of incredulity. They may be true; and even if false, good breeding forces you to hear them with polite attention, and the appearance of belief. To show by word or sign any token of incredulity, is to give the lie to the narrator, and that is an unpardonable insult.

———◦◦◦———

N EED I say that no gentleman will ever soil his mouth with an oath. Above all, to swear in a drawing room or before ladies is not only indelicate and vulgar in the extreme, but evinces a shocking ignorance of the rules of polite society and good breeding.

A VOID a declamatory style; some men, before speaking, will wave their hands as if commanding silence, and, having succeeded in obtaining the attention of the company, will speak in a tone, and style, perfectly suitable for the theatre or lecture room, but entirely out of place in a parlour. Such men entirely defeat the object of society, for they resent interruption, and, as their talk flows in a constant stream, no one else can speak without interrupting the pompous idiot who thus endeavours to engross the entire attention of the circle around him. This character will be met with constantly, and generally joins to the other disagreeable traits an egotism as tiresome as it is ill-bred.

A VOID set phrases, and use quotations but rarely. They sometimes make a very piquant addition to conversation, but when they become a constant habit, they are exceedingly tedious, and in bad taste.

V ULGAR language and slang, though in common, unfortunately too common use, are unbecoming in anyone who pretends to be a gentleman. Many of the words heard now in the parlour and drawing room, derive their origin from sources which a gentleman would hesitate to mention before ladies, yet he will make daily use of the offensive word or phrase.

B E careful in society never to play the part of buffoon, for you will soon become known as the 'funny' man of the party, and no character is so perilous to your dignity as a gentleman. You lay yourself open to both censure and ridicule, and you may feel sure that, for every person who laughs with you, two are laughing at you, and for one who admires you, two will watch your antics with secret contempt.

W HILE refusing the part of jester yourself, do not, by stiff manners, or cold, contemptuous looks, endeavour to check the innocent mirth of others. It is in excessively bad taste to drag in a grave subject of conversation when pleasant, bantering talk is going on around you. Join in pleasantly and forget your graver thoughts for the time, and you will win more popularity than if you chill the merry circle or turn their innocent gaiety to grave discussions.

I T is extremely rude and pedantic, when engaged in general conversation, to make quotations in a foreign language.

T O use phrases which admit of a double meaning, is ungentlemanly, and, if addressed to a lady, they become positively insulting.

I F you find you are becoming angry in a conversation, either turn to another subject or keep silence. You may utter, in the heat of passion, words which you would never use in a calmer moment, and which you would bitterly repent when they were once said.

'N EVER talk of ropes to a man whose father was hanged' is a vulgar but popular proverb. Avoid carefully subjects which may be construed into personalities, and keep a strict reserve upon family matters. Avoid, if you can, seeing the skeleton in your friend's closet, but if it is paraded for your special benefit, regard it as a sacred confidence, and never betray your knowledge to a third party.

I F you have travelled, although you will endeavour to improve your mind in such travel, do not be constantly speaking of your journeyings. Nothing is more tiresome than a man who commences every phrase with, 'When I was in Paris', or, 'In Italy I saw —'.

W HEN asking questions about persons who are not known to you, in a drawing room, avoid using adjectives; or you may enquire of a mother, 'Who is that awkward, ugly girl?' and be answered, 'Sir, that is my daughter.'

A VOID gossip; in a woman it is detestable, but in a man it is utterly despicable.

———≈◈≈———

D O not officiously offer assistance or advice in general society. Nobody will thank you for it.

———≈◈≈———

A LADY of sense will feel more complimented if you converse with her upon instructive, high subjects, than if you address to her only the language of compliment. In the latter case she will conclude that you consider her incapable of discussing higher subjects, and you cannot expect her to be pleased at being considered merely a silly, vain person, who must be flattered into good humour.

———≈◈≈———

I T is a somewhat ungrateful task to tell those who would shrink from the imputation of a falsehood that they are in the daily habit of uttering untruths; and yet, if I proceed, no other course than this can be taken by me. It is of no use to adopt half measures; plain speaking saves a deal of trouble.

———≈◈≈———

T HE examples about to be given by me of exaggerated expressions, are only a few of the many that are constantly in use. Whether you can acquit yourselves of the charge of occasionally using them, I cannot tell; but I dare not affirm for myself that I am altogether guiltless.

'I was caught in the wet last night, the rain came down in torrents.' Most of us have been out in heavy rains; but a torrent of water pouring down from the skies would a little surprise us, after all.

'I am wet to the skin, and have not a dry thread upon me.' Where these expressions are once used correctly, they are used twenty times in opposition to the truth.

'I tried to overtake him, but in vain; for he ran like lightning.' The celebrated racehorse Eclipse is said to have run a mile in a minute, but poor Eclipse is left sadly behind by this expression.

'He kept me standing out in the cold so long, I thought I should have waited forever.' There is not a particle of probability that such a thought could have been for one moment entertained.

'As I came across the common, the wind was as keen as a razor.' This is certainly a very keen remark, but the worst of it is that its keenness far exceeds its correctness.

'I went to the meeting, but had hard work to get in; for the place was crowded to suffocation.' In this case, in justice to the veracity of the relater, it is necessary to suppose that successful means had been used for his recovery.

'It must have been a fine sight; I would have given the world to have seen it.' Fond as most of us are of sight-seeing, this would be buying pleasure at a dear price indeed; but it is an easy thing to proffer to part with that which we do not possess.

'It made me quite low-spirited; my heart felt as heavy as lead.' We most of us know what a heavy heart is; but lead is by no means the most correct metaphor to use in speaking of a heavy heart.

'I could hardly find my way, for the night was as dark as pitch.' I am afraid we have all in our turn calumniated the sky in this manner; pitch is many shades darker than the darkest night we have ever known.

'I have told him of that fault fifty times over.' Five times would, in all probability, be much nearer the fact than fifty.

'I never closed my eyes all night long.' If this be true, you acted unwisely; for had you closed your eyes, you might, perhaps, have fallen asleep, and enjoyed the blessing of refreshing slumber; if it be not true, you acted more unwisely still, by stating that as a fact which is altogether untrue.

'He is as tall as a church-spire.' I have met with some tall fellows in my time, though the spire of a church is somewhat taller than the tallest of them.

'You may buy a fish at the market as big as a jackass, for five shillings.' I certainly have my doubts about this matter; but if it be really true, the market people must be jackasses indeed to sell such large fishes for so little money.

'He was so fat he could hardly come in at the door.' Most likely the difficulty here alluded to was never felt by anyone but the relater; supposing it to be otherwise, the man must have been very broad or the door very narrow.

'You don't say so! – why, it was enough to kill him!' The fact that it did not kill him is a sufficient reply to this unfounded observation; but no remark can be too absurd for an unbridled tongue.'

———◦◎◦———

THUS might I run on for an hour, and after all leave much unsaid on the subject of exaggerated expressions. We are hearing continually the comparisons, 'black as soot, white as snow, hot as fire, cold as ice, sharp as a needle, dull as a door-nail, light as a feather, heavy as lead, stiff as a poker, and crooked as a crab-tree,' in cases where such expressions are quite out of order.

———◦◎◦———

THE practice of expressing ourselves in this inflated and thoughtless way, is more mischievous than we are aware of. It certainly leads us to sacrifice truth; to misrepresent what we mean faithfully to describe; to whiten our own characters, and sometimes to blacken the reputation of a neighbour. There is an uprightness in speech as well as in action, that we ought to strive hard to attain. The purity of truth is sullied, and the standard of integrity is lowered, by incorrect observations. Let us reflect upon this matter freely and faithfully. Let us love truth, follow truth, and practise truth in our thoughts, our words, and our deeds.

CHAPTER II

Politeness

R EAL politeness is the outward expression of the most
generous impulses of the heart. It enforces unselfishness, benevolence, kindness, and the golden rule, 'Do unto
others as you would others should do unto you.' Thus its first
principle is love for the neighbour, loving him as yourself.

W HEN in society it would often be exceedingly difficult
to decide how to treat those who are personally disagreeable to us, if it were not for the rules of politeness, and
the little formalities and points of etiquette which these rules
enforce. These evidences of polite breeding do not prove
hypocrisy, as you may treat your most bitter enemy with
perfect courtesy, and yet make no protestations of friendship.

I F politeness is but a mask, as many philosophers tell us, it
is a mask which will win love and admiration, and is better
worn than cast aside. If you wear it with the sincere desire
to give pleasure to others, and make all the little meetings
of life pass off smoothly and agreeably, it will soon cease to

be a mask, but you will find that the manner which you at first put on to give pleasure, has become natural to you, and wherever you have assumed a virtue to please others, you will find the virtue becoming habitual and finally natural, and part of yourself.

D O not look upon the rules of etiquette as deceptions. They are just as often vehicles for the expression of sincere feeling, as they are the mask to conceal a want of it.

Y OU will in society meet with men who rail against politeness, and call it deceit and hypocrisy. Watch these men when they have an object to gain, or are desirous of making a favourable impression, and see them tacitly, but unconsciously, admit the power of courtesy, by dropping for the time, their uncouth ways, to affect the politeness they oftentimes do not feel.

P ASS over the defects of others, be prudent, discreet, at the proper time reserved, yet at other times frank, and treat others with the same gentle courtesy you would wish extended to yourself.

T RUE politeness never embarrasses anyone, because its first object is to put all at their ease, while it leaves to all perfect freedom of action. You must meet rudeness from others by perfect politeness and polish of manner on your own part, and you will thus shame those who have been uncivil to you. You will more readily make them blush by your courtesy, than if you met their rudeness by ill manners on your own part.

WHILE a favour may be doubled in value, by a frankly courteous manner of granting it, a refusal will lose half its bitterness if your manner shows polite regret at your inability to oblige him who asks the favour at your hand.

POLITENESS may be extended to the lowest and meanest, and you will never by thus extending it detract from your own dignity. A *gentleman* may and will treat his washerwoman with respect and courtesy, and his boot-black with pleasant affability, yet preserve perfectly his own position. To really merit the name of a polite, finished gentleman, you must be polite at all times and under all circumstances.

THERE is a difference between politeness and etiquette. Real politeness is inborn, and may exist in the savage, while etiquette is the outward expression of politeness reduced to the rules current in good society.

A MAN may be polite, really so in heart, yet show in every movement an ignorance of the rules of etiquette, and offend against the laws of society. You may find him with his elbows upon the table, or tilting his chair in a parlour. You may see him commit every hour gross breaches of etiquette, yet you will never hear him intentionally utter one word to wound another, you will see that he habitually endeavours to make others comfortable, choosing for them the easiest seats, or the daintiest dishes, and putting self entirely aside to contribute to the pleasure of all around him. Such a man will learn, by contact with refined society, that his ignorance of the rules which govern it, make him, at times, disagreeable, and from the same unselfish motive which prompts him to make a sacrifice of comfort for the sake of others, he will watch and learn quickly, almost by instinct, where he offends against good breeding, drop one by one his errors in etiquette, and become truly a gentleman.

O N the other hand, you will meet constantly, in the best society, men whose polish of manner is exquisite, who will perform to the minutest point the niceties of good breeding, who never commit the least act that is forbidden by the strictest rules of etiquette; yet under all this mask of chivalry, gallantry, and politeness will carry a cold, selfish heart; will, with a sweet smile, graceful bow, and elegant language, wound deeply the feelings of others, and while passing in society for models of courtesy and elegance of manner, be in feeling as cruel and barbarous as the veriest savage.

S o I would say to you, cultivate your heart. Cherish there the Christian graces, love for the neighbour, unselfishness, charity, and gentleness, and you will be truly a gentleman; add to these the graceful forms of etiquette, and you then become a *perfect* gentleman.

———❧———

E tiquette exists in every corner of the known world, from the savages in the wilds of Africa, who dare not, upon penalty of death, approach their barbarous rulers without certain forms and ceremonies, to the most refined circles of Europe, where gentle chivalry and a cultivated mind suggest its rules. It has existed in all ages, and the stringency of its laws in some countries has given rise to both ludicrous and tragic incidents.

———❧———

I n countries where royalty rules the etiquette, it often happens that pride will blind those who make the rules, and the results are often fatal. Believing that the same deference which their rank authorised them to demand, was also due to them as individuals, the result of such an idea was an etiquette as vain and useless as it was absurd.

———❧———

A t almost all times, and in almost all places, good breeding may be shown; and we think a good service will be done by pointing out a few plain and simple instances in which it stands opposed to habits and manners, which, though improper and disagreeable, are not very uncommon.

I N a public assembly of any kind, a well-bred man will pay regard to the feelings and wishes of the females by whom he is surrounded. He will not secure the best seat for himself, and leave the womenfolk to take care of themselves. He will not be seated at all, if the meeting be crowded, and a single female appear unaccommodated.

G OOD breeding will keep a person from making loud and startling noises, from pushing past another in entering or going out of a room; from ostentatiously using a pocket-handkerchief; from hawking and spitting in company; from fidgeting any part of the body; from scratching the head, or picking the teeth with fork or with finger. In short, it will direct all who study its rules to abstain from every personal act which may give pain or offence to another's feelings. At the same time, it will enable them to bear much without taking offence. It will teach them when to speak and when to be silent, and how to behave with due respect to all. By attention to the rules of good breeding, and more especially to its leading prin-ciples, the poorest man will be entitled to the character of a gentleman, and by inattention to them, the most wealthy person will be essentially vulgar. Vulgarity signifies coarseness or indelicacy of manner, and is not necessarily associated with poverty or lowliness of condition. Thus an operative artisan may be a gentleman, and worthy of our particular esteem; while an opulent merchant may be only a vulgar clown, with whom it is impossible to be on terms of friendly intercourse.

Iₙ the familiar intercourse of society, a well-bred *man* will be known by the delicacy and deference with which he behaves towards females. That man would deservedly be looked upon as very deficient in proper respect and feeling, who should take any physical advantage of one of the weaker sex, or offer any personal slight towards her. Woman looks, and properly looks, for protection to man. It is the province of the husband to shield the wife from injury; of the father to protect the daughter; the brother has the same duty to perform towards the sister; and, in general, every man should, in this sense, be the champion and the lover of every woman. Not only should he be ready to protect, but desirous to please, and willing to sacrifice much of his own personal ease and comfort, if, by doing so, he can increase those of any female in whose company he may find himself.

CHAPTER III

Table Etiquette

I T may seem a very simple thing to eat your meals, yet there is no occasion upon which the gentleman, and the low-bred, vulgar man are more strongly contrasted, than when at the table. The rules I shall give for table etiquette when in company will apply equally well for the home circle, with the exception of some few points, readily discernible, which may be omitted at your own table.

A WELL-BRED man, receiving an invitation to dine with a friend, should reply to it immediately, whether he accepts or declines it.

H E should be punctual to the hour named in the invitation, five or ten minutes earlier if convenient, but not one instant later. He must never, unless he has previously asked permission to do so, take with him any friend not named in his invitation. His host and hostess have the privilege of inviting whom they will, and it is an impertinence to force them to extend their hospitality, as they must do if you introduce a friend at their own house.

S PEAK, on entering the parlour of your friend, first to the hostess, then to the host.

W HEN dinner is announced, the host or hostess will give the signal for leaving the drawing room, and you will probably be requested to escort one of the ladies to the table. Offer to her your left arm, and at the table wait until she is seated, indeed wait until every lady is seated, before taking your own place.

I N leaving the parlour you will pass out first, and the lady will follow you, still holding your arm. At the door of the dining room, the lady will drop your arm. Pass in, then wait on one side of the entrance till she passes you, to her place at the table.

I F there are no ladies, you may go to the table with any gentleman who stands near you, or with whom you may be conversing when dinner is announced. If your companion is older than yourself, extend to him the same courtesy which you would use towards a lady.

I F, when at home, you practise habitually the courtesies of the table, they will sit upon you easily when abroad; but if you neglect them at home, you will use them awkwardly when in company, and you will find yourself recognised as a man who has 'company manners', only when abroad.

———◦◦◦———

I HAVE seen men who eat soup, or chew their food, in so noisy a manner as to be heard from one end of the table to the other; fill their mouths so full of food, as to threaten suffocation or choking; use their own knife for the butter, and salt; put their fingers in the sugar bowl; and commit other faults quite as monstrous, yet seem perfectly unconscious that they were doing anything to attract attention.

———◦◦◦———

T RY to sit easily and gracefully, but at the same time avoid crowding those beside you.

———◦◦◦———

F AR from eating with avidity of whatever delicacies which may be upon the table, and which are often served in small quantities, partake of them but sparingly, and decline them when offered the second time.

———◦◦◦———

M ANY men at their own table have little peculiar notions, which a guest does well to respect. Some will feel hurt, even offended, if you decline a dish which they recommend; while others expect you to eat enormously, as if they feared you did not appreciate their hospitality unless you tasted of every dish upon the table. Try to pay respect to such whims at the table of others, but avoid having any such notions when presiding over your own board.

O BSERVE a strict sobriety; never drink of more than one kind of wine, and partake of that sparingly.

T HE style of serving dinner is different at different houses; if there are many servants they will bring you your plate filled, and you must keep it. If you have the care of a lady, see that she has what she desires, before you give your own order to the waiter; but if there are but few domestics, and the dishes are upon the table, you may with perfect propriety help those near you, from any dish within your reach.

I F your host or hostess passes you a plate, keep it, especially if you have chosen the food upon it, for others have also a choice, and by passing it, you may give your neighbour dishes distasteful to him, and take yourself those which he would much prefer.

I F in the leaves of your salad, or in a plate of fruit you find a worm or insect, pass your plate to the waiter, without any comment, and he will bring you another.

B E careful to avoid the extremes of gluttony or over-dain-
tiness at table. To eat enormously is disgusting; but if
you eat too sparingly, your host may think that you despise
his fare.

B EFORE taking your place at table, wait until your place
is pointed out to you, unless there are cards bearing the
names of the guests upon the plates; in the latter case, take
the place thus marked for you.

P UT your napkin upon your lap, covering your knees. It
is out of date, and now looked upon as a vulgar habit to
put your napkin up over your breast.

S IT neither too near nor too far from the table. Never
hitch up your coat-sleeves or wristbands as if you were
going to wash your hands. Some men do this habitually, but
it is a sign of very bad breeding.

N EVER tip your chair, or lounge back in it during dinner.

A LL gesticulations are out of place, and in bad taste at the table. Avoid making them.

———◦⟨⊙⟩◦———

C ONVERSE in a low tone to your neighbour, yet not with any air of secrecy if others are engaged in *tête-à-tête* conversation; if, however, the conversation is general, avoid conversing *tête-à-tête*. Do not raise your voice too much; if you cannot make those at some distance from you hear you when speaking in a moderate tone, confine your remarks to those near you.

———◦⟨⊙⟩◦———

I F you wish for a knife, plate, or anything from the side table, never address those in attendance as 'Waiter!' as you would at a hotel or *restaurant*, but call one of them by name; if you cannot do this, make him a sign without speaking.

———◦⟨⊙⟩◦———

N EVER blow your soup if it is too hot, but wait until it cools. Never raise your plate to your lips, but eat with your spoon.

———◦⟨⊙⟩◦———

N EVER touch either your knife or your fork until after you have finished eating your soup. Leave your spoon in your soup plate, that the servant may remove them both. Never take soup twice.

———◦⟨⊙⟩◦———

I N changing your plate, or passing it during dinner, remove your knife and fork, that the plate *alone* may be taken, but after you have finished your dinner, cross the knife and fork on the plate, that the servant may take all away, before bringing you clean ones for dessert.

———⟨◦⟩———

D O not bite your bread from the roll or slice, nor cut it with your knife; break off small pieces and put these in your mouth with your fingers.

———⟨◦⟩———

A T dinner do not put butter on your bread. Never dip a piece of bread into the gravy or preserves upon your plate and then bite it, but if you wish to eat them together, break the bread into small pieces, and carry these to your mouth with your fork.

———⟨◦⟩———

W ATCH that the lady whom you escorted to the table is well helped. Lift and change her plate for her, pass her bread, salt, and butter, give her orders to the waiter, and pay her every attention in your power.

———⟨◦⟩———

N EVER criticise any dish before you.

———⟨◦⟩———

N EVER eat so fast as to hurry the others at the table, nor so slowly as to keep them waiting.

——◦◦◦——

U SE always the salt-spoon, sugar-tongs, and butter knife; to use your own knife, spoon, or fingers, evinces a shocking want of good-breeding.

——◦◦◦——

I F a dish is distasteful to you, decline it, but make no remarks about it. It is sickening and disgusting to explain at a table how one article makes you sick, or why some other dish has become distasteful to you. I have seen a well-dressed tempting dish go from a table untouched, because one of the company told a most disgusting anecdote about finding vermin served in a similar dish. No wit in the narration can excuse so palpably an error of politeness.

——◦◦◦——

N EVER put bones, or the seeds of fruit upon the table-cloth. Put them upon the edge of your plate.

——◦◦◦——

N EVER use your knife for any purpose but to *cut* your food. It is not meant to be put in your mouth. Your fork is intended to carry the food from your plate to your mouth, and no gentleman ever eats with his knife.

——◦◦◦——

I F the meat or fish upon your plate is too rare or too well-done, do not eat it; give for an excuse that you prefer some other dish before you; but never tell your host that his cook has made the dish uneatable.

N EVER speak when you have anything in your mouth. Never pile the food on your plate as if you were starving, but take a little at a time; the dishes will not run away.

N EVER put fruit or bonbons in your pocket to carry them from the table.

I F you wish to remove a fish bone or fruit seed from your mouth, cover your lips with your hand or napkin, that others may not see you remove it.

I F you wish to use your handkerchief, and have not time to leave the table, turn your head away, and as quickly as possible put the handkerchief in your pocket again.

A LWAYS wipe your mouth before drinking, as nothing is more ill-bred than to grease your glass with your lips.

I F you are invited to drink with a friend, and do not drink wine, bow, raise your glass of water and drink with him.

D O not propose to take wine with your host; it is his privilege to invite you.

D O not put your glass upside down on the table to signify that you do not wish to drink any more; it is sufficient to refuse firmly. Do not be persuaded to touch another drop of wine after your own prudence warns you that you have taken enough.

A VOID any air of mystery when speaking to those next you; it is ill-bred and in excessively bad taste.

I F you wish to speak of anyone, or to anyone at the table, call them by name, but never point or make a signal when at table.

W HEN taking coffee, never pour it into your saucer, but let it cool in the cup, and drink from that.

O N leaving the table put your napkin on the table, but do not fold it.

O FFER your arm to the lady whom you escorted to the table.

I T is excessively rude to leave the house as soon as dinner is over. Respect to your hostess obliges you to stay in the drawing room at least an hour.

I F the ladies withdraw, leaving the gentlemen, after dinner, rise when they leave the table, and remain standing until they have left the room.

CHAPTER IV

————◦◦◦◦————

Etiquette in the Street

A GENTLEMAN will be always polite, in the parlour, dining room, and in the street. This last clause will especially include courtesy towards ladies, no matter what may be their age or position. A man who will annoy or insult a woman in the street, lowers himself to a brute, no matter whether he offends by look, word, or gesture. There are several little forms of etiquette, given below, the observance of which will mark the gentleman in the street.

————◦◦◦◦————

WHEN walking with a lady, or with a gentleman who is older than yourself, give them the upper side of the pavement, that is, the side nearest the house.

————◦◦◦◦————

WHEN walking alone, and you see anyone coming towards you on the same side of the street, give the upper part of the pavement, as you turn aside, to a man who may carry a heavy bundle, to a priest or clergyman, to a woman, or to any elderly person.

———⊙⊙⊙———

I N a crowd never rudely push aside those who impede your progress, but wait patiently until the way is clear. If you are hurried by business of importance or an engagement, you will find that a few courteous words will open the way before you more quickly than the most violent pushing and loud talking.

———⊙⊙⊙———

I F obliged to cross a plank, or narrow path, let any lady or old person who may also be passing, precede you. In case the way is slippery or in any way unsafe, you may, with perfect propriety, offer to assist either a lady or elderly person in crossing it.

———⊙⊙⊙———

B E careful about your dress. You can never know whom you may meet, so it is best to never leave the house otherwise than well dressed. Bright colours, and much jewelry are both unbecoming to a gentleman in the street.

———⊙⊙⊙———

A VOID touching any one with your elbows in passing, and do not swing your arms as you walk.

———⊙⊙⊙———

D O not smoke in the street until after dark, and then remove your cigar from your mouth, if you meet a lady.

B E careful when walking with or near a lady, not to put your foot upon her dress.

I N carrying an umbrella, hold it so that you can see the way clear before you; avoid striking your umbrella against those which pass you; if you are walking with a lady, let the umbrella cover her perfectly, but hold it so that you will not touch her bonnet. If you have the care of two ladies, let them carry the umbrella between them, and walk outside yourself. Nothing can be more absurd than for a gentleman to walk between two ladies, holding the umbrella himself; while, in this way, he is perfectly protected, the ladies receive upon their dresses and cloaks the little streams of water which run from the points of the umbrella.

I N case of a sudden fall of rain, you may, with perfect propriety, offer your umbrella to a lady who is unprovided with one. If she accepts it, and asks your address to return it, leave it with her; if she hesitates, and does not wish to deprive you of the use of it, you may offer to accompany her to her destination, and then, do not open a conversation; let your manner be respectful, and when you leave her, let her thank you, assure her of the pleasure it has given you to be of service, bow, and leave her.

IN meeting a lady friend, wait for her to bow to you, and in returning her salutation, remove your hat. To a gentleman you may bow, merely touching your hat, if he is alone or with another gentleman; but if he has a lady with him, raise your hat in bowing to him. If you stop to speak to a lady, hold your hat in your hand, until she leaves you, unless she requests you to replace it. With a gentleman you may replace it immediately.

———❦———

YOU may bow to a lady who is seated at a window, if you are in the street; but you must not bow from a window to a lady in the street.

———❦———

DO not stop to join a crowd who are collected round a street show, or street merchant, unless you wish to pass for a countryman taking a holiday in the city.

———❦———

IF you stop anyone to enquire your own way, or if you are called upon to direct another, remove your hat while asking or answering the question.

———❦———

IF you see a lady leaving a carriage unattended, or hesitating at a bad crossing, you may, with propriety, offer your hand or arm to assist her, and having seen her safely upon the pavement, bow, and pass on.

———⋅◦⦿◦⋅———

I N a car or omnibus, when a lady wishes to get out, stop the car for her, pass up her fare, and in an omnibus alight and assist her in getting out, bowing as you leave her.

———⋅◦⦿◦⋅———

B E gentle, courteous, and kind to children. There is no surer token of a low, vulgar mind, than unkindness to little ones whom you may meet in the streets.

———⋅◦⦿◦⋅———

A TRUE gentleman never stops to consider what may be the position of any woman whom it is in his power to aid in the street. The true spirit of chivalry makes the courtesy due to the sex, not to the position of the individual.

———⋅◦⦿◦⋅———

W HEN you are escorting a lady in the street, politeness does not absolutely require you to carry her bundle or parasol, but if you are gallant you will do so. You must regulate your walk by hers, and not force her to keep up with your ordinary pace.

———⋅◦⦿◦⋅———

I F you are walking in the country, and pass any streamlet, offer your hand to assist your companion in crossing.

———⋅◦⦿◦⋅———

IF you pass over a fence, and she refuses your assistance in crossing it, walk forward, and do not look back, until she joins you again. The best way to assist a lady over a fence, is to stand yourself upon the upper rail, and while using one hand to keep a steady position, stoop, offer her the other, and with a firm, steady grasp, hold her hand until she stands beside you; then let her go down on the other side first, and follow her when she is safe upon the ground.

―――❦―――

IN starting for a walk with a lady, unless she is a stranger in the place towards whom you act as guide, let her select your destination.

―――❦―――

WHERE there are several ladies, and you are required to escort one of them, select the elderly, or those whose personal appearance will probably make them least likely to be sought by others. You will probably be repaid by finding them very intelligent, and with a fund of conversation. If there are more ladies than gentlemen, you may offer an arm to two, with some jest about the difficulty of choosing, or the double honour you enjoy.

―――❦―――

OFFER your seat in any public conveyance, to a lady who is standing.

―――❦―――

WHEN with a lady you must pay her expenses as well as your own; if she offers to share the expense, decline unless she insists upon it, in the latter case yield gracefully. Many ladies, who have no brother or father, and are dependent upon their gentlemen friends for escort, make it a rule to be under no pecuniary obligations to them, and you will, in such a case, offend more by insisting upon your right to take that expense, than by quietly pocketing your dignity and their cash together. I know many gentlemen will cry out at my assertion; but I have observed this matter, and know many *ladies* who will sincerely agree with me in my opinion.

NEVER put your arm across the seat, or around her, as many do in riding. It is an impertinence, and if she is a lady of refinement, she will resent it as such.

BE the last to enter the carriage, the first to leave it. If you have ladies with you, offer them your hand to assist them in entering and alighting, and you should take the arm of an old gentleman to assist him.

IF offered a seat in the carriage of a gentleman friend, stand aside for him to get in first, but if he waits for you, bow and take your seat before he does.

WHEN driving a lady in a two-seated vehicle, you should assist her to enter the carriage, see that her dress is not in danger of touching the wheels, and that her shawl, parasol, and fan, are where she can reach them, before you take your own seat. If she wishes to stop, and you remain with the horses, you should alight before she does, assist her in alighting, and again alight to help her to her seat when she returns, even if you keep your place on the seat whilst she is gone.

WHEN attending a lady in a horseback ride, never mount your horse until she is ready to start. Give her your hand to assist her in mounting, arrange the folds of her habit, hand her her reins and her whip, and then take your own seat on your saddle.

LET her pace be yours. Start when she does, and let her decide how fast or slowly she will ride. Never let the head of your horse pass the shoulders of hers, and be watchful and ready to render her any assistance she may require.

NEVER, by rapid riding, force her to ride faster than she may desire.

NEVER touch her bridle, reins, or whip, except she particularly requests your assistance, or an accident, or threatened danger, makes it necessary.

IF the road is muddy be careful that you do not ride so as to bespatter her habit. It is best to ride on the side away from that upon which her habit falls. Some ladies change their side in riding, from time to time, and you must watch and see upon which side the skirt falls, that, on a muddy day, you may avoid favouring the habit with the mud your horse's hoofs throw up.

IF you ride with a gentleman older than yourself, or one who claims your respect, let him mount before you do. Extend the same courtesy towards any gentleman whom you have invited to accompany you, as he is, for the ride, your guest.

THE honourable place is on the right. Give this to a lady, an elderly man, or your guest.

CHAPTER V

Etiquette for Calling

A GENTLEMAN in society must calculate to give a certain portion of his time to making calls upon his friends, both ladies and gentlemen. He may extend his visiting list to as large a number as his inclination and time will permit him to attend to, but he cannot contract it after passing certain limits. His position as a man in society obliges him to call,

Upon any stranger visiting his city, who brings a letter of introduction to him;

Upon any friend from another city, to whose hospitality he has been at any time indebted;

Upon any gentleman after receiving from his hands a favour or courtesy;

Upon his host at any dinner or supper party (such calls should be made very soon after the entertainment given);

Upon any friend whose joy or grief calls for an expression of sympathy, whether it be congratulation or condolence;

Upon any friend who has lately returned from a voyage or long journey;

Upon any lady who has accepted his services as an escort, either for a journey or the return from a ball or evening party; this call must be made the day after he has thus escorted the lady;

Upon his hostess after any party to which he has been invited, whether he has accepted or declined such invitation;

Upon any lady who has accepted his escort for an evening, a walk or a drive;

Upon any friend whom long or severe illness keeps confined to the house;

Upon his lady friends on New Year's day (if it is the custom of the city in which he resides);

Upon any of his friends when they receive bridal calls;

Upon lady friends in any city you are visiting; if gentlemen friends reside in the same city, you may either call upon them or send your card with your address and the length of time you intend staying, written upon it; if a stranger or friend visiting your city sends such a card, you must call at the earliest opportunity;

Upon anyone of whom you wish to ask a favour; to make him, under such circumstances call upon you, is extremely rude;

Upon anyone who has asked a favour of you; you will add very much to the pleasure you confer, in granting a favour, by calling to express the gratification it affords you to be able to oblige your friend; you will soften the pain of a refusal, if, by calling, and expressing your regret, you show that you feel interested in the request, and consider it of importance.

Upon intimate friends, relatives, and ladies, you may call without waiting for any of the occasions given above.

Do not fall into the vulgar error of declaiming against the practice of making calls, declaring it a 'bore', tiresome, or stupid. The custom is a good one.

Any first call which you receive must be returned promptly. If you do not wish to continue the acquaintance any farther, you need not return a second call, but politeness imperatively demands a return of the first one.

A call may be made upon ladies in the morning or afternoon; but in this country, where almost every man has some business to occupy his day, the evening is the best time for paying calls. You will gain ground in easy intercourse and friendly acquaintance more rapidly in one evening, than in several morning calls.

———❦———

NEVER make a call upon a lady before eleven o'clock in the morning, or after nine in the evening.

———❦———

AVOID meal times. If you inadvertently call at dinner or tea time, and your host is thus forced to invite you to the table, it is best to decline the civility. If, however, you see that you will give pleasure by staying, accept the invitation, but be careful to avoid calling again at the same hour.

———❦———

'VISITING,' says a French writer, 'forms the cord which binds society together, and it is so firmly tied, that were the knot severed, society would perish.'

———❦———

IF you see the master of the house take letters or a paper from his pocket, look at the clock, have an absent air, beat time with his fingers or hands, or in any other way show weariness or *ennui*, you may safely conclude that it is time for you to leave, though you may not have been five minutes in the house. If you are host to the most wearisome visitor in existence, if he stays hours, and converses only on subjects which do not interest you, in the least, unless he is keeping you from an important engagement, you must not show the least sign of weariness. Listen to him politely, endeavour to entertain him, and preserve a smiling composure, though you may long to show him the door. In case he is keeping you from business of importance, or an imperative engagement, you may, without any infringement upon the laws of politeness, inform him of the fact, and beg him to excuse you; you must, however, express polite regret at your enforced want of hospitality, and invite him to call again.

IT is quite an art to make a graceful exit after a call. To know how to choose the moment when you will be regretted, and to retire leaving your friends anxious for a repetition of the call, is an accomplishment worth acquiring.

WHEN you begin to tire of your visit, you may generally feel sure that your entertainers are tired of you, and if you do not want to remain printed upon their memory as 'the man who makes such long, tiresome calls', you will retire.

IF other callers come in before you leave a friend's parlour, do not rise immediately as if you wished to avoid them, but remain seated a few moments, and then leave, that your hostess may not have too many visitors to entertain at one time.

IF you have been enjoying a *tête-à-tête* interview with a lady, and other callers come in, do not hurry away, as if detected in a crime, but after a few courteous, graceful words, and the interchange of some pleasant remarks, leave her to entertain her other friends.

———◦◦◦———

To endeavour when making a call to 'sit out' others in the room, is very rude.

———◦◦◦———

When your host or hostess urges you to stay longer, after you have risen to go, be sure that that is the best time for departure. You will do better to go then, when you will be regretted, than to wait until you have worn your welcome out.

———◦◦◦———

When making a visit of condolence, take your tone from your host or hostess. If they speak of their misfortune, or, in case of death, of the departed relative, join them. Speak of the talents or virtues of the deceased, and your sympathy with their loss. If, on the other hand, they avoid the subject, then it is best for you to avoid it too. They may feel their inability to sustain a conversation upon the subject of their recent affliction, and it would then be cruel to force it upon them. If you see that they are making an effort, perhaps a painful one, to appear cheerful, try to make them forget for the time their sorrows, and chat on cheerful subjects. At the same time, avoid jesting, merriment, or undue levity, as it will be out of place, and appear heartless.

———◦◦◦———

A visit of congratulation, should, on the contrary, be cheerful, gay, and joyous. Here, painful subjects would be out of place. Do not mar the happiness of your friend by the description of the misery of your own position or that of a third person, but endeavour to show by joyous sympathy that the pleasure of your friend is also your happiness. To laugh with those who laugh, weep with those who are afflicted, is not hypocrisy, but kindly, friendly sympathy.

————⟡————

ALWAYS, when making a friendly call, send up your card, by the servant who opens the door.

————⟡————

THERE are many times when a card may be left, even if the family upon which you call is at home. Visits of condolence, unless amongst relatives or very intimate friends, are best made by leaving a card with enquiries for the health of the family, and offers of service.

————⟡————

IF you see upon entering a friend's parlour, that your call is keeping him from going out, or, if you find a lady friend dressed for a party or promenade, make your visit very brief. In the latter case, if the lady seems unattended, and urges your stay, you may offer your services as an escort.

————⟡————

NEVER visit a literary man, an artist, any man whose profession allows him to remain at home, at the hours when he is engaged in the pursuit of his profession. The fact that you know he is at home is nothing; he will not care to receive visits during the time allotted to his daily work.

THE calls made after receiving an invitation to dinner, a party, ball, or other entertainment should be made within a fortnight after the civility has been accepted.

WHEN you have saluted the host and hostess, do not take a seat until they invite you to do so, or by a motion, and themselves sitting down, show that they expect you to do the same.

KEEP your hat in your hand when making a call. This will show your host that you do not intend to remain to dine or sup with him. You may leave an umbrella or cane in the hall if you wish, but your hat and gloves you must carry into the parlour. In making an evening call for the first time keep your hat and gloves in your hand, until the host or hostess requests you to lay them aside and spend the evening.

WHEN going to spend the evening with a friend whom you visit often, leave your hat, gloves, and great coat in the hall.

WHEN you find, on entering a room, that your visit is for any reason inopportune, do not instantly retire unless you have entered unperceived and can so leave, in which case leave immediately; if, however, you have been seen, your instant retreat is cut off. Then endeavour by your own graceful ease to cover any embarrassment your entrance may have caused, make but a short call, and, if you can, leave your friends under the impression that you saw nothing out of the way when you entered.

ALWAYS leave a card when you find the person upon whom you have called absent from home.

A CARD should have nothing written upon it, but your name and address. To leave a card with your business address, or the nature of your profession written upon it, shows a shocking ignorance of polite society. Business cards are never to be used excepting when you make a business call.

NEVER use a card that is ornamented in any way, whether by a fancy border, painted corners, or embossing. Let it be perfectly plain, tinted, if you like, in colour, but without ornament, and have your name written or printed in the middle, your address, in smaller characters, in the lower left hand corner. Many gentlemen omit the Mr upon their cards, writing merely their Christian and surname; this is a matter of taste, you may follow your own inclination. Let your card be written thus:

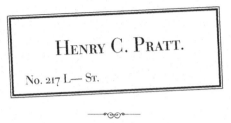

HENRY C. PRATT.

No. 217 L— St.

I F you call upon a lady, who invites you to be seated, place a chair for her, and wait until she takes it before you sit down yourself.

I F a lady enters the room where you are making a call, rise, and remain standing until she is seated. Even if she is a perfect stranger, offer her a chair, if there is none near her.

I F you are engaged in any profession which you follow at home, and receive a caller, you may, during the daytime, invite him into your library, study, or the room in which you work, and, unless you use your pen, you may work while he is with you.

W HEN you receive a visitor, meet him at the door, offer a chair, take his hat and cane, and, while speaking of the pleasure the call affords you, show, by your manner, that you are sincere, and desire a long call.

D<small>O</small> not let your host come with you any farther than the room door if he has other visitors; but if you are showing out a friend, and leave no others in the parlour, you should come to the street door.

CHAPTER VI

Etiquette for the Ballroom

O F all the amusements open for young people, none is more delightful and more popular than dancing. Lord Chesterfield, in his letters to his son, says: 'Dancing is, in itself, a very trifling and silly thing; but it is one of those established follies to which people of sense are sometimes obliged to conform; and then they should be able to do it well. And, though I would not have you a dancer, yet, when you do dance, I would have you dance well, as I would have you do everything you do well.' In another letter, he writes: 'Do you mind your dancing while your dancing master is with you? As you will be often under the necessity of dancing a minuet, I would have you dance it very well. Remember that the graceful motion of the arms, the giving of your hand, and the putting off and putting on of your hat genteelly, are the material parts of a gentleman's dancing. But the greatest advantage of dancing well is, that it necessarily teaches you to present yourself, to sit, stand, and walk genteelly; all of which are of real importance to a man of fashion.'

A LTHOUGH the days are over when gentlemen carried their hats into ballrooms and danced minuets, there are useful hints in the quotations given above. Nothing will give ease of manner and a graceful carriage to a gentleman more surely than the knowledge of dancing. He will, in its practice, acquire easy motion, a light step, and learn to use both hands and feet well. What can be more awkward than a man who continually finds his hands and feet in his way, and, by his fussy movements, betrays his trouble? A good dancer never feels this embarrassment, consequently he never appears aware of the existence of his feet, and carries his hands and arms gracefully. Some people being bashful and afraid of attracting attention in a ballroom or evening party, do not take lessons in dancing, overlooking the fact that it is those who do *not* partake of the amusement on such occasions, not those who do, that attract attention. To all such gentlemen I would say: learn to dance. You will find it one of the very best plans for correcting bashfulness. Unless you possess the accomplishments that are common in polite society, you can neither give nor receive all the benefits that can be derived from social intercourse.

WHEN you receive an invitation to a ball, answer it immediately.

IF you go alone, go from the dressing room to the ballroom, find your host and hostess, and speak first to them; if there are several ladies in the house, take the earliest opportunity of paying your respects to each of them, and invite one of them to dance with you the first dance. If she is already engaged, you should endeavour to engage her for a dance later in the evening, and are then at liberty to seek a partner amongst the guests.

WHEN you have engaged a partner for a dance, you should go to her a few moments before the set for which you have engaged her will be formed, that you may not be hurried in taking your places upon the floor. Enquire whether she prefers the head or side place in the set, and take the position she names.

IN inviting a lady to dance with you, the words, 'Will you *honour* me with your hand for a quadrille?' or, 'Shall I have the *honour* of dancing this set with you?' are more used now than 'Shall I have the *pleasure*?' or, 'Will you give me the *pleasure* of dancing with you?'

OFFER a lady your arm to lead her to the quadrille, and in the pauses between the figures endeavour to make the duty of standing still less tiresome by pleasant conversation. Let the subjects be light, as you will be constantly interrupted by the figures in the dance. There is no occasion upon which a pleasant flow of small talk is more *àpropos*, and agreeable than in a ballroom.

W HEN the dance is over, offer your arm to your partner, and enquire whether she prefers to go immediately to her seat, or wishes to promenade. If she chooses the former, conduct her to her seat, stand near her a few moments, chatting, then bow, and give other gentlemen an opportunity of addressing her. If she prefers to promenade, walk with her until she expresses a wish to sit down. Enquire, before you leave her, whether you can be of any service, and, if the supper-room is open, invite her to go in there with you.

Y OU will pay a delicate compliment and one that will certainly be appreciated, if, when a lady declines your invitation to dance on the plea of fatigue or fear of fatigue, you do not seek another partner, but remain with the lady you have just invited, and thus imply that the pleasure of talking with, and being near, her, is greater than that of dancing with another.

L ET your hostess understand that you are at her service for the evening, that she may have a prospect of giving her wall flowers a partner, and, however unattractive these may prove, endeavour to make yourself as agreeable to them as possible.

Y OUR conduct will differ if you escort a lady to a ball. Then your principal attentions must be paid to her. You must call for her punctually at the hour she has appointed, and it is your duty to provide the carriage. You may carry her a bouquet if you will, this is optional. A more elegant way of presenting it is to send it in the afternoon with your card, as, if you wait until evening, she may think you do not mean to present one, and provide one for herself.

———⁂———

WHEN you arrive at your destination, leave the carriage, and assist her in alighting; then escort her to the ladies' dressing room, leave her at the door, and go to the gentlemen's dressing room. As soon as you have arranged your own dress, go again to the door of the ladies' room, and wait until your companion comes out. Give her your left arm and escort her to the ballroom; find the hostess and lead your companion to her. When they have exchanged greetings, lead your lady to a seat, and then engage her for the first dance. Tell her that while you will not deprive others of the pleasure of dancing with her, you are desirous of dancing with her whenever she is not more pleasantly engaged, and before seeking a partner for any other set, see whether your lady is engaged or is ready to dance again with you. You must watch during the evening, and, while you do not force your attentions upon her, or prevent others from paying her attention, you must never allow her to be alone, but join her whenever others are not speaking to her. You must take her in to supper, and be ready to leave the party, whenever she wishes to do so.

———⁂———

IF the ball is given in your own house, or at that of a near relative, it becomes your duty to see that every lady, young or old, handsome or ugly, is provided with a partner, though the oldest and ugliest may fall to your own share.

—◦◦◦—

NEVER stand up to dance unless you are perfect master of the step, figure, and time of that dance. If you make a mistake you not only render yourself ridiculous, but you annoy your partner and the others in the set.

—◦◦◦—

WHEN you conduct your partner to her seat, thank her for the pleasure she has conferred upon you, and do not remain too long conversing with her.

—◦◦◦—

GIVE your partner your whole attention when dancing with her. To let your eyes wander round the room, or to make remarks betraying your interest in others, is not flattering, as she will not be unobservant of your want of taste.

—◦◦◦—

BE very careful not to forget an engagement. It is an unpardonable breach of politeness to ask a lady to dance with you, and neglect to remind her of her promise when the time to redeem it comes.

—◦◦◦—

A DRESS coat, dress boots, full suit of black, and white or very light kid gloves must be worn in a ballroom. A white waistcoat and cravat are sometimes worn, but this is a matter of taste.

———⋅⊙⊙⋅°———

I F one lady refuses you, do not ask another who is seated near her to dance the same set. Do not go immediately to another lady, but chat a few moments with the one whom you first invited, and then join a group or gentlemen friends for a few moments, before seeking another partner.

———⋅⊙⊙⋅°———

N EVER dance without gloves. This is an imperative rule. It is best to carry two pairs, as in the contact with dark dresses, or in handing refreshments, you may soil the pair you wear on entering the room, and will thus be under the necessity of offering your hand covered by a soiled glove, to some fair partner. You can slip unperceived from the room, change the soiled for a fresh pair, and then avoid that mortification.

———⋅⊙⊙⋅°———

I F your partner has a bouquet, handkerchief, or fan in her hand, do not offer to carry them for her. If she finds they embarrass her, she will request you to hold them for her, but etiquette requires you not to notice them, unless she speaks of them first.

———⋅⊙⊙⋅°———

D O not be the last to leave the ballroom. It is more elegant to leave early, as staying too late gives others the impression that you do not often have an invitation to a ball, and must 'make the most of it'.

Some gentlemen linger at a private ball until all the ladies have left, and then congregate in the supper-room, where they remain for hours, totally regardless of the fact that they are keeping the wearied host and his servants from their rest. Never, as you value your reputation as a gentleman of refinement, be among the number of these 'hangers on'.

CHAPTER VII

Dress

BETWEEN the sloven and the coxcomb there is generally a competition which shall be the more contemptible: the one in the total neglect of everything which might make his appearance in public supportable, and the other in the cultivation of every superfluous ornament. The former offends by his negligence and dirt, and the latter by his finery and perfumery. Each entertains a supreme contempt for the other, and while both are right in their opinion, both are wrong in their practice. It is not in either extreme that the man of real elegance and refinement will be shown, but in the happy medium which allows taste and judgement to preside over the wardrobe and toilet-table, while it prevents too great an attention to either, and never allows personal appearance to become the leading object of life.

THE French have a proverb, 'It is not the cowl which makes the monk', and it might be said with equal truth, 'It is not the dress which makes the gentleman', yet, as the monk is known abroad by his cowl, so the true gentleman will let the refinement of his mind and education be seen in his dress.

T HE first rule for the guidance of a man, in matters of dress, should be, 'Let the dress suit the occasion'. It is as absurd for a man to go into the street in the morning with his dress-coat, white kid gloves, and dancing-boots, as it would be for a lady to promenade the fashionable streets, in full evening dress, or for the same man to present himself in the ballroom with heavy walking-boots, a great coat, and riding-cap.

I T is true that there is little opportunity for a gentleman to exercise his taste for colouring, in the black and white dress which fashion so imperatively declares to be the proper dress for a *dress* occasion. He may indulge in light clothes in the street during the warm months of the year, but for the ball or evening party, black and white are the only colours (or no colours) admissible, and in the midst of the gay dresses of the ladies, the unfortunate man in his sombre dress appears like a demon who has found his way into Paradise among the angels. *N'importe!* Men should be useful to the women, and how can they better employed than acting as a foil for their loveliness of face and dress!

N OTWITHSTANDING the dress, however, a man may make himself agreeable, even in the earthly Paradise, a ballroom. He can rise above the mourning of his coat, to the joyousness of the occasion, and make himself valued for himself, not his dress. He can make himself admired for his wit, not his toilette; his elegance and refinement, not the price of his clothes.

———❦———

T HERE is another good rule for the dressing room: While you are engaged in dressing give your whole attention to it. See that every detail is perfect, and that each article is neatly arranged. From the curl of your hair to the tip of your boot, let all be perfect in its make and arrangement, but, as soon as you have left your mirror, forget your dress. Nothing betokens the coxcomb more decidedly than to see a man always fussing about his dress, pulling down his wristbands, playing with his moustache, pulling up his shirt collar, or arranging the bow of his cravat. Once dressed, do not attempt to alter any part of your costume until you are again in the dressing room.

———❦———

I N a gentleman's dress any attempt to be conspicuous is in excessively bad taste. If you are wealthy, let the luxury of your dress consist in the fine quality of each article, and in the spotless purity of gloves and linen, but never wear much jewellery or any article conspicuous on account of its money value. Simplicity should always preside over the gentleman's wardrobe.

———❦———

F OLLOW fashion as far as is necessary to avoid eccentricity or oddity in your costume, but avoid the extreme of the prevailing *mode*. If coats are worn long, yours need not sweep the ground, if they are loose, yours may still have some fitness for your figure; if pantaloons are cut large over the boot, yours need not cover the whole foot, if they are tight, you may still take room to walk. Above all, let your figure and style of face have some weight in deciding how far you are to follow fashion. For a very tall man to wear a high, narrow-brimmed hat, long-tailed coat, and tight pantaloons, with a pointed beard and hair brushed up from the forehead, is not more absurd than for a short, fat man, to promenade the street in a low, broad-brimmed hat, loose coat and pants, and the latter made of large plaid material, and yet burlesques quite as broad may be met with every day.

An English writer, ridiculing the whims of Fashion, says: –

'To be in the fashion, an Englishman must wear six pairs of gloves in a day:

In the morning, he must drive his hunting wagon in reindeer gloves.

In hunting, he must wear gloves of chamois skin.

To enter London in his tilbury, beaver skin gloves.

Later in the day, to promenade in Hyde Park, coloured kid gloves, dark.

When he dines out, coloured kid gloves, light.

For the ballroom, white kid gloves.'

Thus his yearly bill for gloves alone will amount to a most extravagant sum.

In order to merit the appellation of a well-dressed man, you must pay attention, not only to the more prominent articles of your wardrobe, coat, pants, and vest, but to the more minute details. A shirtfront which fits badly, a pair of wristbands too wide or too narrow, a badly brushed hat, a shabby pair of gloves, or an ill-fitting boot, will spoil the most elaborate costume. Purity of skin, teeth, nails; well-brushed hair; linen fresh and snowy white, will make clothes of the coarsest material, if well made, look more elegant, than the finest material of cloth, if these details are neglected.

Frequent bathing, careful attention to the teeth, nails, ears, and hair, are indispensable to a finished toilette.

Use but very little perfume, much of it is in bad taste.

Let your hair, beard, and moustache, be always perfectly smooth, well arranged, and scrupulously clean.

I T is better to clean the teeth with a piece of sponge, or very soft brush, than with a stiff brush, and there is no dentifrice so good as White Castile Soap.

W EAR always gloves and boots, which fit well and are fresh and whole. Soiled or torn gloves and boots ruin a costume otherwise faultless.

E XTREME propriety should be observed in dress. Be careful to dress according to your means. Too great saving is meanness, too great expense is extravagance.

A YOUNG man may follow the fashion farther than a middle-aged or elderly man, but let him avoid going to the extreme of the mode, if he would not be taken for an empty-headed fop.

I T is best to employ a good tailor, as a suit of coarse broad-cloth which fits you perfectly, and is stylish in cut, will make a more elegant dress than the finest material badly made.

A void eccentricity; it marks, not the man of genius, but the fool.

———⚬⊙⚬———

A well brushed hat, and glossy boots must be always worn in the street.

———⚬⊙⚬———

W hite gloves are the only ones to be worn with full dress.

———⚬⊙⚬———

A snuff box, watch, studs, sleeve-buttons, watch-chain, and one ring are all the jewellery a well-dressed man can wear.

———⚬⊙⚬———

A n English author, in a recent work, gives the following rules for a gentleman's dress:

'The best bath for general purposes, and one which can do little harm, and almost always some good, is a sponge bath. It should consist of a large, flat metal basin, some four feet in diameter, filled with cold water. Such a vessel may be bought for about fifteen shillings. A large, coarse sponge – the coarser the better – will cost another five or seven shillings, and a few Turkish towels complete the "properties". The water should be plentiful and fresh, that is, brought

up a little while before the bath is to be used; not
placed over night in the bedroom. Let us wash and
be merry, for we know not how soon the supply of
that precious article which here costs nothing may
be cut off. In many continental towns they buy their
water, and on a protracted sea voyage the ration is
often reduced to half a pint a day *for all purposes*,
so that a pint per diem is considered luxurious.
Seawater, we may here observe, does not cleanse,
and a sensible man who bathes in the sea will take
a bath of pure water immediately after it. This
practice is shamefully neglected, and I am inclined
to think that in many cases a sea-bath will do more
harm than good without it, but, if followed by a
fresh bath, cannot but be advantageous.'

───◦◦◦◦───

'THE ancients followed up the bath by anointing the
body, and athletic exercises. The former is a mistake;
the latter, an excellent practice, shamefully neglected in the
present day. It would conduce much to health and strength
if every morning toilet comprised the vigorous use of the
dumb-bells, or, still better, the exercise of the arms without
them. The best plan of all is, to choose some object in your
bed-room on which to vent your hatred, and box at it violently
for some ten minutes, till the perspiration covers you. The
sponge must then be again applied to the whole body. It is
very desirable to remain without clothing as long as possible,
and I should therefore recommend that every part of the
toilet which can conveniently be performed without dressing,
should be so.'

'THE next duty, then, must be to clean the teeth. Dentists are modern inquisitors, but their torture-rooms are meant only for the foolish. Everybody is born with good teeth, and everybody might keep them good by a proper diet, and the avoidance of sweets and smoking. Of the two the former are, perhaps, the more dangerous. Nothing ruins the teeth so soon as sugar in one's tea, and highly sweetened tarts and puddings, and as it is *le premier pas qui coûte*, these should be particularly avoided in childhood. When the teeth attain their full growth and strength it takes much more to destroy either their enamel or their substance.'

'THE teeth should be well rubbed inside as well as outside, and the back teeth even more than the front. The mouth should then be rinsed, if not seven times, according to the Hindu legislator, at least several times, with fresh, cold water. This same process should be repeated several times a day, since eating, smoking, and so forth, naturally render the teeth and mouth dirty more or less, and nothing can be so offensive, particularly to ladies, whose sense of smell seems to be keener than that of the other sex, and who can detect at your first approach whether you have been drinking or smoking.'

'STRICT attention must be paid to the condition of the nails, and that both as regards cleaning and cutting. The former is best done with a liberal supply of soap on a small nail-brush, which should be used before every meal, if you would not injure your neighbour's appetite. While the hand is still moist, the point of a small pen-knife or pair of stumpy nail-scissors should be passed under the nails so as to remove every vestige of dirt; the skin should be pushed down with a towel, that the white half-moon may be seen, and the finer skin removed with the knife or scissors. Occasionally the edges of the nails should be filed, and the hard skin which forms round the corners of them cut away. The important point in cutting the nails is to preserve the beauty of their shape. That beauty, even in details, is worth preserving, I have already remarked, and we may study it as much in paring our nails, as in the grace of our attitudes, or any other point. The shape, then, of the nail should approach, as nearly as possible, to the oblong. The length of the nail is an open question. Let it be often cut, but always long, in my opinion. Above all, let it be well cut, and *never* bitten.'

'THE person who invented razors libelled Nature, and added a fresh misery to the days of man.'

'WHATEVER *Punch* may say, the moustache and beard movement is one in the right direction, proving that men are beginning to appreciate beauty and to acknowledge that Nature is the best valet. But it is very amusing to hear men excusing their vanity on the plea of health, and find them indulging in the hideous "Newgate frill" as a kind of compromise between the beard and the razor. There was a time when it was thought a presumption and vanity to wear one's own hair instead of the frightful elaborations of the wig-makers, and the false curls which Sir Godfrey Kneller did his best to make graceful on canvas. Who knows that at some future age some *Punch* of the twenty-first century may not ridicule the wearing of one's own teeth instead of the dentist's? At any rate Nature knows best, and no man need be ashamed of showing his manhood in the hair of his face. Of razors and shaving, therefore, I shall only speak from necessity, because, until everybody is sensible on this point, they will still be used.'

'NAPOLEON shaved himself. "A born king," said he, "has another to shave him. A made king can use his own razor." But the war he made on his chin was very different to that he made on foreign potentates. He took a very long time to effect it, talking between whiles to his hangers-on. The great man, however, was right, and every sensible man will shave himself, if only as an exercise of character, for a man should learn to live, in every detail without assistance. Moreover, in most cases, we shave ourselves better than barbers can do. If we shave at all, we should do it thoroughly, and every morning. Nothing, except a frown and a hay-fever, makes the face look so unlovely as a chin covered with short stubble. The chief requirements are hot water, a large, soft brush of badger hair, a good razor, soft soap that will not dry rapidly, and a steady hand. Cheap razors are a fallacy. They soon lose their edge, and no amount of stropping will restore it. A good razor needs no strop. If you can afford it, you should have a case of seven razors, one for each day of the week, so that no one shall be too much used.'

'BEARDS, moustaches, and whiskers, have always been most important additions to the face. In the present day literary men are much given to their growth, and in that respect show at once their taste and their vanity. Let no man be ashamed of his beard, if it be well kept and not fantastically cut. The moustache should be kept within limits. The style of the beard should be adopted to suit the face. A broad face should wear a large, full one; a long face is improved by a sharp-pointed one. Taylor, the water poet, wrote verses on the various styles, and they are almost numberless. The chief point is to keep the beard well combed and in neat trim.'

'As to whiskers, it is not every man who can achieve a pair of full length. There is certainly a great vanity about them, but it may be generally said that foppishness should be avoided in this as in most other points. Above all, the whiskers should never be curled, nor pulled out to an absurd length. Still worse is it to cut them close with the scissors. The moustache should be neat and not too large, and such fopperies as cutting the points thereof, or twisting them up to the fineness of needles – though patronised by the Emperor of the French – are decidedly a proof of vanity. If a man wear the hair on his face which nature has given him, in the manner that nature distributes it, keeps it clean, and prevents its overgrowth, he cannot do wrong. All extravagances are vulgar, because they are evidence of a pretence to being better than you are; but a single extravagance unsupported is perhaps worse than a number together, which have at least the merit of consistency. If you copy puppies in the half-yard of whisker, you should have their dress and their manner too, if you would not appear doubly absurd.'

———⁕৹৹৹৹⁕———

'THE same remarks apply to the arrangement of the hair in men, which should be as simple and as natural as possible, but at the same time a little may be granted to beauty and the requirements of the face. For my part I can see nothing unmanly in wearing long hair, though undoubtedly it is inconvenient and a temptation to vanity, while its arrangement would demand an amount of time and attention which is unworthy of a man.'

———⁕৹৹৹৹⁕———

'IF we conform to fashion we should at least make the best of it, and since the main advantage of short hair is its neatness, we should take care to keep ours neat. This should be done first by frequent visits to the barber, for if the hair is to be short at all it should be very short, and nothing looks more untidy than long, stiff, uncurled masses sticking out over the ears. If it curls naturally so much the better, but if not it will be easier to keep in order. The next point is to wash the head every morning, which, when once habitual, is a great preservative against cold. A pair of large brushes, hard or soft, as your case requires, should be used, not to hammer the head with, but to pass up under the hair so as to reach the roots. As to pomatum, Macassar, and other inventions of the hair-dresser, I have only to say that, if used at all, it should be in moderation, and never sufficiently to make their scent perceptible in company. Of course the arrangement will be a matter of individual taste, but as the middle of the hair is the natural place for a parting, it is rather a silly prejudice to think a man vain who parts his hair in the centre. He is less blamable than one who is too lazy to part it at all, and has always the appearance of having just got up.'

———

'THIS brings me to speak of certain necessities of dress; the first of which I shall take is appropriateness. The age of the individual is an important consideration in this respect; and a man of sixty is as absurd in the style of nineteen as a young man in the high cravat of Brummell's day. We may, therefore, give as a general rule, that after the turning-point of life a man should eschew the changes of fashion in his own attire, while he avoids complaining of it in the young. In the latter, on the other hand, the observance of these changes must depend partly on his taste and partly on his position. If wise, he will adopt with alacrity any new fashions which improve the grace, the ease, the healthfulness, and the convenience of his garments.'

———

'POSITION in society demands appropriateness. Well knowing the worldly value of a good coat, I would yet never recommend a man of limited means to aspire to a fashionable appearance. In the first place, he becomes thereby a walking falsehood; in the second, he cannot, without running into debt, which is another term for dishonesty, maintain the style he has adopted. As he cannot afford to change his suits as rapidly as fashion alters, he must avoid following it in varying details. In general, it may be said that there is vulgarity in dressing like those of a class above us, since it must be taken as a proof of pretension.'

'As it is bad taste to flaunt the airs of the town among the provincials, who know nothing of them, it is worse taste to display the dress of a city in the quiet haunts of the rustics. The law, that all attempts at distinction by means of dress is vulgar and pretentious, would be sufficient argument against wearing city fashions in the country.'

'While in most cases a rougher and easier mode of dress is both admissible and desirable in the country, there are many occasions of country visiting where a town man finds it difficult to decide. It is almost peculiar to the country to unite the amusements of the daytime with those of the evening; of the open air with those of the drawing-room. Thus, in the summer, when the days are long, you will be asked to a picnic or an archery party, which will wind up with dancing indoors, and may even assume the character of a ball. If you are aware of this beforehand, it will always be safe to send your evening dress to your host's house, and you will learn from the servants whether others have done the same, and whether, therefore, you will not be singular in asking leave to change your costume. But if you are ignorant how the day is to end, you must be guided partly by the hour of invitation, and partly by the extent of your intimacy with the family.'

'ANOTHER requisite in dress is its simplicity, with which I may couple harmony of colour. This simplicity is the only distinction which a man of taste should aspire to in the matter of dress, but a simplicity in appearance must proceed from a nicety in reality. One should not be simply ill dressed, but simply well dressed. Lord Castlereagh would never have been pronounced the most distinguished man in the gay court of Vienna, because he wore no orders or ribbons among hundreds decorated with a profusion of those vanities, but because besides this he was dressed with taste. The charm of Brummell's dress was its simplicity; yet it cost him as much thought, time, and care as the portfolio of a minister. The rules of simplicity, therefore, are the rules of taste. All extravagance, all splendour, and all profusion must be avoided. The colours, in the first place, must harmonise both with our complexion and with one another; perhaps most of all with the colour of our hair. All bright colours should be avoided, such as red, yellow, sky-blue, and bright green. Perhaps only a successful Australian gold digger would think of choosing such colours for his coat, waistcoat, or trousers; but there are hundreds of young men who might select them for their gloves and neck-ties. The deeper colours are, somehow or other, more manly, and are certainly less striking.'

'JEWELS are an ornament to women, but a blemish to men. They bespeak either effeminacy or a love of display. The hand of a man is honoured in working, for labour is his mission; and the hand that wears its riches on its fingers, has rarely worked honestly to win them. The best jewel a man can wear is his honour. Let that be bright and shining, well set in prudence, and all others must darken before it. But as we are savages, and must have some silly trickery to hang about us, a little, but very little concession may be made to our taste in this respect.'

———⸎———

'THE man of good taste will wear as little jewellery as possible. One handsome signet-ring on the little finger of the left hand, a scarf-pin which is neither large, nor showy, nor too intricate in its design, and a light, rather thin watch-guard with a cross-bar, are all that he ought to wear.'

———⸎———

'THE precious stones are reserved for ladies, and even our scarf-pins are more suitable without them.'

———⸎———

'THE dress that is both appropriate and simple can never offend, nor render its wearer conspicuous, though it may distinguish him for his good taste. But it will not be pleasing unless clean and fresh. We cannot quarrel with a poor gentleman's thread-bare coat, if his linen be pure, and we see that he has never attempted to dress beyond his means or unsuitably to his station. But the sight of decayed gentility and dilapidated fashion may call forth our pity, and, at the same time prompt a moral: "You have evidently sunken," we say to ourselves. While freshness is essential to being well dressed, it will be a consolation to those who cannot afford a heavy tailor's bill, to reflect that a visible newness in one's clothes is as bad as patches and darns, and to remember that there have been celebrated dressers who would never put on a new coat till it had been worn two or three times by their valets. On the other hand, there is no excuse for untidiness, holes in the boots, a broken hat, torn gloves, and so on. Indeed, it is better to wear no gloves at all than a pair full of holes. There is nothing to be ashamed of in bare hands, if they are clean, and the poor can still afford to have their shirts and shoes mended, and their hats ironed. It is certainly better to show signs of neatness than the reverse, and you need sooner be ashamed of a hole than a darn.'

'CHANGE your linen whenever it is at all dirty.'

'THIS is the best guide with regard to collars, socks, pocket-handkerchiefs, and our under garments. No rule can be laid down for the number we should wear per week, for everything depends on circumstances. Thus in the country all our linen remains longer clean than in town; in dirty, wet, or dusty weather, our socks get soon dirty and must be changed; or, if we have a cold, to say nothing of the possible but not probable case of tear-shedding on the departure of friends, we shall want more than one pocket-handkerchief per diem.'

'A WELL-DRESSED man does not require so much an extensive as a varied wardrobe. He wants a different costume for every season and every occasion; but if what he selects is simple rather than striking, he may appear in the same clothes as often as he likes, as long as they are fresh and appropriate to the season and the object. There are four kinds of coats which he must have: a morning-coat, a frock-coat, a dress-coat, and an over-coat. An economical man may do well with four of the first, and one of each of the others per annum. The dress of a gentleman in the present day should not cost him more than the tenth part of his income on an average. But as fortunes vary more than position, if his income is large it will take a much smaller proportion, if small a larger one. If a man, however, mixes in society, and I write for those who do so, there are some things which are indispensable to even the proper dressing, and every occasion will have its proper attire.'

'THEN, too, there is a scale of honour among clothes, which must not be forgotten. Thus, a new coat is more honourable than an old one, a cut-away or shooting-coat than a dressing-gown, a frock-coat than a cut-away, a dark blue frock-coat than a black frock-coat, a tail-coat than a frock-coat. There is no honour at all in a blue tail-coat, however, except on a gentleman of eighty, accompanied with brass buttons and a buff waistcoat. There is more honour in an old hunting-coat than in a new one, in a uniform with a bullet hole in it than one without, in a fustian jacket and smock-frock than in a frock-coat, because they are types of labor, which is far more honourable than lounging. Again, light clothes are generally placed above dark ones, because they cannot be so long worn, and are, therefore, proofs of expenditure, *alias* money, which in this world is a commodity more honoured than every other; but, on the other hand, tasteful dress is always more honourable than that which has only cost much. Light gloves are more esteemed than dark ones, and the prince of glove-colours is, undeniably, lavender.'

CHAPTER VIII

Manly Exercises

BODILY exercise is one of the most important means provided by nature for the maintenance of health, and in order to prove the advantages of exercise, we must show what is to be exercised, why exercise is necessary, and the various modes in which it may be taken.

THE human body may be regarded as a wonderful machine, the various parts of which are so wonderfully adapted to each other, that if one be disturbed all must suffer. The bones and muscles are the parts of the human frame on which motion depends. There are four hundred muscles in the body; each one has certain functions to perform, which cannot be disturbed without danger to the whole. They assist the tendons in keeping the bones in their places, and put them in motion. Whether we walk or run, sit or stoop, bend the arm or head, or chew our food, we may be said to open and shut a number of hinges, or ball and socket joints. And it is a wise provision of nature, that, to a certain extent, the more the muscles are exercised, the stronger do they become; hence it is that labourers and artisans are stronger and more muscular than those persons whose lives are passed in easy occupations or professional duties.

———◦◦◦———

B ESIDES strengthening the limbs, muscular exercise has a most beneficial influence on respiration and the circulation of the blood. The larger blood-vessels are generally placed deep among the muscles, consequently when the latter are put into motion, the blood is driven through the arteries and veins with much greater rapidity than when there is no exercise; it is more completely purified, as the action of the insensible perspiration is promoted, which relieves the blood of many irritating matters, chiefly carbonic acid and certain salts, taken up in its passage through the system, and a feeling of lightness and cheerfulness is diffused over body and mind.

———◦◦◦———

W E have said that a good state of health depends in a great measure on the proper exercise of *all the muscles*. But on looking at the greater portion of our industrial population, – artisans and workers in factories generally – we find them, in numerous instances, standing or sitting in forced or unnatural positions, using only a few of their muscles, while the others remain, compara- tively speaking, unused or inactive. Sawyers, filers, tailors, and many others may be easily recognised as they walk the streets, by the awkward movement and bearing impressed upon them by long habit. The stooping position especially tells most fatally upon the health; weavers, shoemakers, and cotton-spinners have generally a sallow and sickly appearance, very different from that of those whose occu- pation does not require them to stoop, or to remain long in a hurtful posture. Their common affections are indigestion and dull headache, with giddiness especially during summer. They attribute their complaints to two causes, one of which is the posture of the body, bent for twelve or thirteen hours a day, the other the heat of the working-room.

———

BESIDES the trades above enumerated, there are many others productive of similar evils by the position into which they compel workmen, or by the close and confined places in which they are carried on; and others, again, in their very natures injurious. Plumbers and painters suffer from the noxious materials which they are constantly using, grinders and filers from dust, and bakers from extremes of temperature and irregular hours. Wherever there is physical depression, there is a disposition to resort to injurious stimulants; and 'the time of relief from work is generally spent, not in invigorating the animal frame, but in aggravating complaints, and converting functional into organic disease'.

———

BUT there are others who suffer from artificial poisons and defective exercise as well as artisans and operatives – the numerous class of shopkeepers; the author above quoted says, 'Week after week passes without affording them one pure inspiration. Often, also, they have not exercise even in the open air of the town; a furlong's walk to church on Sunday being the extent of their rambles. When they have the opportunity they want the inclination for exercise. The father is anxious about his trade or his family, the mother is solicitous about her children. Each has little taste for recreation or amusement.' The various disorders, generally known under the name of indigestion, disorders dependent on a want of circulation of blood through the bowels, biliary derangements, and headache, are well known to be the general attendants on trade, closely pursued. Indeed, in almost every individual, this absorbing principle produces one or other of the various maladies to which I have alluded.

————◦⊚◦————

THE great remedy for the evils here pointed out is bodily exercise, of some kind, every day, and as much as possible in the open air. An opinion prevails that an occasional walk is sufficient to maintain the balance of health; but if the intervals of inaction be too long, the good effect of one walk is lost before another is taken. Regularity and sufficiency are to be as much regarded in exercise as in eating or sleeping. Sir James Clark says, that 'the exercise which is to benefit the system generally, must be in the open air, and extend to the whole muscular system. Without regular exercise out of doors, no young person can continue long healthy; and it is the duty of parents in fixing their children at boarding schools to ascertain that sufficient time is occupied daily in this way. They may be assured that attention to this circumstance is quite as essential to the moral and physical health of their children, as any branch of education which they may be taught.'

————◦⊚◦————

EXERCISE, however, must be regulated by certain rules, the principal of which is, to avoid carrying it to excess

– to proportion it always to the state of health and habit of the individual. Persons of short breath predisposed to determination of blood to the head, subject to palpitation of the heart, or general weakness, are not to believe that a course of severe exercise will do them good; on the contrary, many serious results often follow over-fatigue. For the same reason it is desirable to avoid active exertion immediately after a full meal, as the foundation of heart diseases is some-times laid by leaping or running after eating. The great object should be so to blend exercise and repose, as to ensure the highest possible amount of bodily vigour. It must be recol-lected that exhausted muscles can be restored only by the most perfect rest.

I N the next place, it is a mistake to consider the labour of the day as equivalent to exercise. Work, generally speaking, is a mere routine process, carried on with but little variety of circumstances, in a confined atmosphere, and in a temperature frequently more exhaustive than restorative. The workman requires something more than this to keep him in health; he must have exercise as often as possible in the open air – in fields, parks, or pleasure grounds; but if these are not at his command, the streets of the town are always open to him, and a walk in these is better than no walk at all. The mere change of scene is beneficial, and in walking he generally sets in motion a different set of muscles from those he has used while at work.

To derive the greatest amount of good from exercise, it must be combined with amusement, and be made pleasurable and recreational. This important fact ought never to be lost sight of, since to ignorance of it alone we owe many of the evils which afflict society. And it would be well if those who have been accustomed to look on social amusements as destructive of the morals of the people, would consider how much good may be done by giving the mind a direction which, while promotive of health, would fill it with cheerfulness and wean it from debasing habits. The character of our sports at the present time, partake but little of the robust and boisterous spirit of our forefathers; but with the refinement of amusements, the opportunity for enjoying them has been grievously diminished. Cheering signs of a better state of things are, however, visible in many quarters, and we trust that the good work will be carried on until the whole of our population shall be in possession of the means and leisure for pleasurable recreation.

———◦⊙◦———

While indulging in the recreational sports which are to restore and invigorate us, we must be mindful of the many points of etiquette and kindness which will do much, if properly attended to, to promote the enjoyment of our exercise, and we propose to review the principal exercises used among us, and to point out in what places the delicate and gentlemanly attention to our companions will do the most to establish, for the person who practises them, the reputation of a polished gentleman.

———◦⊙◦———

RIDING

THERE are no amusements, probably, which give us so wide a scope for the rendering of attention to a friend as riding and driving. Accompanied, as we may be at any time, by timid companions, the power to convince them, by the management of the horse we ride, and the watch kept at the same time on theirs, that we are competent to act the part of companion and guardian, will enable us to impart to them a great degree of reliance on us, and will, by lessening their fear do much to enhance the enjoyment of the excursion.

WITH ladies, in particular, a horseman cannot be too careful to display a regard for the fears of their companions, and by a constant watch on all the horses in the cavalcade, to show at once his ability and willingness to assist his companions.

THERE are few persons, comparatively speaking, even among those who ride often, who can properly assist a lady in mounting her horse. An over-anxiety to help a lady as gracefully as possible, generally results in a nervous trembling effort which is exceedingly disagreeable to the lady, and, at the same time, dangerous; for were the horse to shy or start, he could not be so easily quieted by a nervous man as by one who was perfectly cool. In the mount the lady must gather her skirt into her left hand, and stand close to the horse, her face toward his head, and her right hand resting on the pommel. The gentleman, having asked permission to assist her, stands at the horse's shoulder, facing the lady, and stooping low, he places his right hand at a proper elevation from the ground. The lady then places her left foot on the gentleman's palm, and as he raises his hand she springs slightly on her right foot, and thus reaches the saddle. The gentleman must not jerk his hand upward, but lift it with a gentle motion. This method of mounting is preferable to a step or horse-block. Keep a *firm* hand, for a sinking foothold will diminish the confidence of a lady in her escort, and, in many cases cause her unnecessary alarm while mounting. To anyone who is likely to be called on to act as cavalier to ladies in horse-back excursions, we would recommend the following practice: saddle a horse with a side saddle, and ask a gentleman friend to put on the skirt of a lady's habit, and with him, practise the mounting and dismounting until you have thoroughly conquered any difficulties you may have experienced at first.

———◦◦◦———

A FTER the seat is first taken by the lady, the gentleman should always stand at the side of the lady's horse until she is firmly fixed in the saddle, has a good foothold on the stirrup, and has the reins and whip well in hand. Having ascertained that his companion is firmly and comfortably fixed in the saddle, the gentleman should mount his horse and take his riding position on the right or 'off' side of the lady's horse, so that, in case of the horse's shying in such a way as to bring him against the other horse, the lady will suffer no inconvenience. In riding with two ladies there are two rules in regard to the gentleman's position.

———◦◦◦◦———

I F both ladies are good riders, they should ride side by side, the ladies to the left; but, if the contrary should be the case, the gentleman should ride *between* the ladies in order to be ready in a moment to assist either in case of one of the horses becoming difficult to manage. Before allowing a lady to mount, the entire furniture of her horse should be carefully examined by her escort. The saddle and girths should be tested to see if they are firm, the stirrup leather examined, in case of the tongue of the buckle being in danger of slipping out by not being well buckled at first, and most particularly the bridle, curb, headstall, and reins should be carefully and thoroughly examined, for on them depends the entire control of the horse. These examinations should never be left to the stable-helps, as the continual harnessing of horses by them often leads to a loose and careless way of attending to such matters, which, though seemingly trivial, may lead to serious consequences.

———◦◦◦◦———

O N the road, the constant care of the gentleman should be to render the ride agreeable to his companion, by the pointing out of objects of interest with which she may not be acquainted, the reference to any peculiar beauty of landscape which may have escaped her notice, and a general lively tone of conversation, which will, if she be timid, draw her mind from the fancied dangers of horseback riding, and render her excursion much more agreeable than if she be left to imagine horrors whenever her horse may prick up his ears or whisk his tail. And, while thus conversing, keep an eye always on the lady's horse, so that in case he should really get frightened, you may be ready by your instruction and assistance to aid the lady in quieting his fears.

———∘☙❦❧∘———

I N dismounting you should offer your right hand to the lady's left, and allow her to use *your* left as a step to dismount on, gently declining it as soon as the lady has left her seat on the saddle, and just before she springs. Many ladies spring from the saddle, but this generally confuses the gentleman and is dangerous to the lady, for the horse *may* move at the instant she springs, which would inevitably throw her backward and might result in a serious injury.

———∘☙❦❧∘———

DRIVING

I N the indulgence of this beautiful pastime there are many points of care and attention to be observed; they will render to the driver himself much gratification by the confidence they will inspire in his companion, by having the knowledge that he or she is being driven by a careful horseman, and thus knowing that half of what danger may attend the pleasure, is removed.

———∘☙❦❧∘———

O N reaching the door of your companion's residence, whom we will suppose to be in this case a lady – though the same attention may well be extended to a gentleman – drive close to the mounting-block or curb, and by heading your horse toward the middle of the road, and slightly backing the wagon, separate the fore and hind wheels on the side next the block as much as possible. This gives room for the lady to ascend into the wagon without soiling her dress by rubbing against either tyre, and also gives the driver room to lean over and tuck into the wagon any part of a lady's dress that may hang out after she is seated.

———⚬⊙⊙⚬———

I N assisting the lady to ascend into the wagon, the best and safest way is to tie the horse firmly to a hitching-post or tree, and then to give to your companion the aid of both your hands; but, in case of there being no post to which you can make the rein fast, the following rule may be adopted:

———⚬⊙⊙⚬———

G RASP the reins firmly with one hand, and draw them just tight enough to let the horse feel that they are held, and with the other hand assist the lady; under *no* circumstances, even with the most quiet horse, should you place a lady in your vehicle without *any* hold on the horse, for, although many horses would stand perfectly quiet, the whole race of them are timid, and any sudden noise or motion may start them, in which case the life of your companion may be endangered. In the light *no-top* or *York* wagon, which is now used almost entirely for pleasure drives, the right hand cushion should always be higher by three or four inches than the left, for it raises the person driving, thus giving him more control, and renders the lady's seat more comfortable and more safe. It is a mistaken idea, in driving, that it shows a perfect horseman, to drive fast. On the contrary, a good horseman is more careful of his horse than a poor one, and in starting, the horse is always allowed to go slowly for time; as he gradually takes up a quicker pace, and becomes warmed up; the driver may push him even to the top of his speed for some distance, always, however, allowing him to slacken his pace toward the end of his drive, and to come to the stopping-place at a moderate gait.

———◦◦◦◦◦———

E NDEAVOUR, by your conversation on the road, to make the ride agreeable to your companion. Never try to show off your driving, but remember, that there is no one who drives with so much apparent ease and so little display as the professional jockey, who, as he devotes his life to the management of the reins, may well be supposed to be the most thoroughly good 'whip'.

———◦◦◦◦◦———

I N helping the lady out of the wagon, the same rule must be observed as in the start; namely, to have your horse well in hand or firmly tied. Should your companion be a gentleman and a horseman, the courtesy is always to offer him the reins, though the offer, if made to yourself by another with whom you are riding, should always be declined; unless, indeed, the horse should be particularly 'hard-mouthed' and your friend's arms should be tired, in which case you should relieve him.

———◦◦◦◦◦———

B E especially careful in the use of the whip, that it may not spring back outside of the vehicle and strike your companion. This rule should be particularly attended to in driving 'tandem' or 'four-in-hand', as a cut with a heavy tandem-whip is by no means a pleasant accompaniment to your drive.

———❦———

BOXING

I N this much-abused accomplishment, there would, from the rough nature of the sport, seem to be small room for civility; yet, in none of the many manly sports is there so great a scope for the exercise of politeness as in this. Should your adversary be your inferior in boxing, there are many ways to teach him and encourage him in his pursuit of proficiency, without knocking him about as if your desire was to injure him as much as possible. And you will find that his gratitude for your forbearance will prompt him to exercise the same indulgence to others who are inferior to himself, and thus by the exchange of gentlemanly civility the science of boxing is divested of one of its most objectionable points, viz: the danger of the combatants becoming angry and changing the sport to a brutal fight.

———❦———

A LWAYS allow your antagonist to choose his gloves from the set, though, if you recommend *any* to him, let him take the hardest ones and you the softest; thus he will receive the easier blows. Allow him the choice of ground and position, and endeavour in every way to give him the utmost chance. In this way, even if you should be worsted in the game, your kindness and courtesy to him will be acknowledged by anyone who may be with you, and by no one more readily than your antagonist himself.

These same rules apply to the art of fencing, the most graceful and beautiful of exercises. Let your opponent have his choice of the foils and sword-gloves, give him the best position for light, and in your thrusts remember that to make a 'hit' does not require you to force your foil as violently as you can against your antagonist's breast; but, that every touch will show if your foils be chalked and the one who has the most 'spots' at the end of the encounter is the beaten man.

⸺◦⟨◦⟩◦⸺

SAILING

WITHIN a few years there has been a most decided movement in favour of aquatic pursuits. Scarcely a town can be found, near the sea or on the bank of a river but what can either furnish a yacht or a barge. In all our principal cities the 'navies' of yachts and barges number many boats. The barge clubs particularly are well fitted with active, healthy men, who can appreciate the physical benefit of a few hours' work at the end of a sixteen-foot sweep, and who prefer health and blistered hands to a life of fashionable and unhealthy amusement. Under the head of sailing we will give some hints of etiquette as to sailing and rowing together. A gentleman will never parade his superiority in these accomplishments, still less boast of it, but rather, that the others may not feel their inferiority, he will keep considerably within his powers. If a guest or a stranger be of the party, the best place must be offered to him, though he may be a bad oar; but, at the same time, if a guest knows his inferiority in this respect, he will, for more reasons than one, prefer an inferior position. So, too, when a certain amount of exertion is required, as in boating, a well-bred man will offer to take the greater share, pull the heaviest oar, and will never shirk his work. In short, the whole rule of good manners on such occasions is not to be selfish, and the most amiable man will therefore be the best bred. It is certainly desirable that a gentleman should be able to handle an oar, or to steer and work a yacht, both that when he has an opportunity he may acquire health, and that he may be able to take part in the charming excursions which are made by water. One rule should apply to all these aquatic excursions, and that is, that the gentleman who invites the ladies, should there be any, and who is, therefore, at the trouble of getting up the party, should always be allowed to steer the boat, unless he decline the post, for he has the advantage of more intimate acquaintance with the ladies, whom he will have to entertain on the trip, and the post of honour should be given him as a compliment to his kindness in undertaking the preliminaries.

HUNTING

O UR hunting field at the 'meet' does not show the gaudy equipment and top-boots of England, but the plain dress of the gentleman farmer, sometimes a blue coat and jockey-cap, but oftener the everyday coat and felt hat, but the etiquette of our hunting field is more observed than in England. There anyone joins the meet, if it is a large one, but here no one enters the field unless acquainted with one or more of the gentlemen on the ground. The rules in the hunt are few and simple. Never attempt to hunt unless you have a fine seat in the saddle and a good horse, and never accept the loan of a friend's horse, still less an enemy's, unless you ride very well. A man may forgive you for breaking his daughter's heart but never for breaking his hunter's neck. Another point is, always to be quiet at a meet, and never join one unless acquainted with someone in the field. Pluck, skill, and a good horse are essentials in hunting. Never talk of your achievements, avoid enthusiastic shouting when you break cover, and do not ride over the hounds. Keep a firm hand, a quick eye, an easy, calm frame of mind, and a good, firm seat on the saddle. Watch the country you are going over, be always ready to help a friend who may 'come to grief', and with the rules and the quiet demeanour you will soon be a favourite in the field.

—⚬⚬⚬—

SKATING

T HOUGH we may, in the cold winter, sigh for the return of spring breezes, and look back with regret on the autumn sports, or even the heat of summer, there is yet a balm for our frozen spirits in the glorious and exhilarating sports of winter. The sleigh filled with laughing female beauties and 'beauties', too, of the sterner sex, and the merry jingle of the bells as we fly along the road or through the streets, are delights of which Old Winter alone is the giver. But, pleasant as the sleigh-ride is, the man who looks for health and exercise at all seasons, turns from the seductive pleasures of the sleigh to the more simple enjoyment derived from the skates. Flying along over the glistening ice to the accompaniment of shouts of merry laughter at some novice's mishap, and feeling that we have within us the speed of the racehorse, the icy pleasure is, indeed, a good substitute for the pleasures of the other seasons.

———◦◦◦———

S o universal has skating become, that instruction in this graceful accomplishment seems almost unnecessary; but, for the benefit of the rising generation who may peruse our work, we will give, from a well-known authority, a few hints as to the manner of using the skates before we add our own instruction as to the etiquette of the skating ground.

———◦◦◦———

'B efore going on the ice, the young skater must learn to put on the skates, and may also learn to walk with them easily in a room, balancing, alternately, on each foot. A skater's dress should be as loose and unencumbered as possible. All fullness of dress is exposed to the wind. As the exercise of skating produces perspiration, flannel next the chest, shoulders, and loins, is necessary to avoid the evils of sudden chills in cold weather.'

———◦◦◦———

'E ither very rough or very smooth ice should be avoided. The person who, for the first time, attempts to skate, must not trust to a stick. He may take a friend's hand for support, if he requires one; but that should be soon relinquished, in order to balance himself. He will, probably, scramble about for half an hour or so, till he begins to find out where the edge of his skate is. The beginner must be fearless, but not violent; nor even in a hurry. He should not let his feet get apart, and keep his heels still nearer together. He must keep the ankle of the foot on the ice quite firm; not attempting to gain the edge of the skate by bending it, because the right mode of getting to either edge is by the inclination of the whole body in the direction required; and this inclination should be made fearlessly and decisively. The leg which is on the ice should be kept perfectly straight; for, though the knee must be somewhat bent at the time of striking, it must be straightened as quickly as possible without any jerk. The leg which is off the ice should also be kept straight, though not stiff, having an easy but straight play, the toe pointing downwards, and the heel from six to twelve inches of the other.'

'THE learner must not look down at the ice, nor at his feet, to see how they perform. He may, at first, incline his body a little forward, for safety, but hold his head up, and see where he goes, his person erect and his face rather elevated than otherwise.'

'WHEN once off, he must bring both feet up together, and strike again, as soon as he finds himself steady enough, rarely allowing both feet to be on the ice together. The position of the arms should be easy and varied; one being always more raised than the other, this elevation being alternate, and the change corresponding to that of the legs; that is, the right arm being raised as the right leg is put down, and vice versa, so that the arm and leg of the same side may not be raised together. The face must be always turned in the direction of the line intended to be described. Hence in backward skating, the head will be inclined much over the shoulder; in forward skating, but slightly. All sudden and violent action must be avoided. Stopping may be caused by slightly bending the knees, drawing the feet together, inclining the body forward, and pressing on the heels. It may be also caused by turning short to the right or left, the foot on the side to which we turn being rather more advanced, and supporting part of the weight.'

———◦◦◦———

WHEN on the ice, if you should get your skates on before your companion, always wait for him; for, nothing is more disagreeable than being left behind on an occasion of this kind. Be ready at all times when skating to render assistance to anyone, either lady or gentleman, who may require it. A *gentleman* may be distinguished at all times by the willingness with which he will give up his sport to render himself agreeable and kind to anyone in difficulty. Should you have one of the skating-sleds so much used for taking ladies on the ice, and should your own ladies, if you are accompanied by any, not desire to use it, the most becoming thing you can do is to place it at the disposal of any other gentleman who has ladies with him, and who is not provided with such a conveyance.

———◦◦◦———

ALWAYS keep to the right in meeting a person on the ice, and always skate perfectly clear of the line in which a lady is advancing, whether she be on skates or on foot.

Attention to the other sex is nowhere more appreciated than on the ice, where they are, unless good skaters, comparatively helpless. Be always prompt to assist in the extrication of anyone who may break through the ice, but let your zeal be tempered by discretion, and always get a rope or ladder if possible, in preference to going near the hole; for there is great risk of your breaking through yourself, and endangering your own life without being able to assist the person already submerged. But should the rope or ladder not be convenient, the best method is to lie flat on your breast on the ice, and push yourself cautiously along until you can touch the person's hand, and then let him climb by it out of the hole.

SWIMMING

S o few persons are unable to swim, that it would be useless for us to furnish any instruction in the actual art of swimming; but a few words on the subject of assisting others while in the water may not come amiss.

I T is a desirable accomplishment to be able to swim in a suit of clothes. This may be practised by good swimmers, cautiously at first, in comparatively shallow water, and afterwards in deeper places. Occasions may frequently occur where it may be necessary to plunge into the water to save a drowning person, where the lack of time, or the presence of ladies, would preclude all possibility of removing the clothes. There are few points of etiquette in swimming, except those of giving all the assistance in our power to beginners, and to remember the fact of our being gentlemen, though the sport may be rough when we are off *terra firma*. We shall therefore devote this section of our exercise department to giving a few general directions as to supporting drowning persons, which support is, after all, the most valued attention we can render to anyone.

I F possible, always go to save a life in company with one or two others. One companion is generally sufficient, but two will do no harm, for, if the service of the second be not required, he can easily swim back to shore. On reaching the object of your pursuit, if he be clinging to anything, caution him, as you approach, to hold it until you tell him to let go, and then to let his arms fall to his side. Then let one of your companions place his hand under the armpit of the person to be assisted, and you doing the like, call to him to let go his support, then tread water until you get his arms on the shoulders of your companion and yourself, and then swim gently to shore. Should you be alone, the utmost you can do is to let him hold his support while you tread water near him until further assistance can be obtained. If you are alone and he has no support, let him rest one arm across your shoulder, put one of your arms behind his back, and the hand under his armpit, and tread water until help arrives. Never let a man in these circumstances *grasp* you in any way, particularly if he be frightened, for you may both be drowned; but, try to cool and reassure him by the intrepidity of your own movements, and he will be safely and easily preserved.

CRICKET

WHEN in the cricket-field, we must allow ourselves to enter into the full spirit of the game; but we must not allow the excitement of the play to make us forget what is due to others and to ourselves. A gentle, easy, and, at the same time, gentlemanly manner, may be assumed. Always offer to your companions the use of your private bat, if they are not similarly provided; for the bats belonging to the club often lose the spring in the handle from constant use, and a firm bat with a good spring will prove very acceptable. In this way you gratify the player, and, as a reward for your kindness, he may, from being well provided, score more for the side than he would with inferior or worn-out tools.

THIS game is more purely democratic than any one we know of, and the most aristocratic of gentlemen takes second rank, for the time, to the most humble cricketer, if the latter be the more skilful. But a good player is not always a gentleman, and the difference in cultivation may always be distinguished. A *gentleman* will never deride anyone for his bad play, nor give vent to oaths, or strong epithets, if disappointed in the playing of one of his side. If he has to ask another player for anything, he does so in a way to establish his claim to gentility. 'May I trouble you for that ball?' or, 'Will you please to hand me that bat?' are much preferable to 'Here, you! ball there!' or, 'Clumsy, don't carry off that bat!' Again, if a gentleman makes a mistake himself, he should always acknowledge it quietly, and never start a stormy discussion as to the merits of his batting or fielding. In fine, preserve the same calm demeanour in the field that you would in the parlour, however deeply you enter into the excitement of the game.

CHAPTER IX

—⁓◦⁓—

Travelling

I N this country where ladies travel so much alone, a gentleman has many opportunities of making this unprotected state a pleasant one. There are many little courtesies which you may offer to a lady when travelling, even if she is an entire stranger to you, and by an air of respectful deference, you may place her entirely at her ease with you, even if you are both young.

—⁓◦⁓—

W HEN travelling with a lady, your duties commence when you are presented to her as an escort. If she is personally a stranger, she will probably meet you at the wharf or car depot; but if an old acquaintance, you should offer to call for her at her residence. Take a hack, and call, leaving ample time for last speeches and farewell tears. If she hands you her purse to defray her expenses, return it to her if you stop for any length of time at a place where she may wish to make purchases. If you make no stop upon your journey, keep the purse until you arrive at your destination, and then return it. If she does not give you the money for her expenses when you start, you had best pay them yourself, keeping an account, and she will repay you at the journey's end.

———◦◦◦◦———

W HEN you start, select for your companion the pleasantest seat, see that her shawl and bag are within her reach, the window lowered or raised as she may prefer, and then leave her to attend to the baggage, or, if you prefer, let her remain in the hack while you get checks for the trunks. Never keep a lady standing upon the wharf or in the depot, whilst you arrange the baggage.

———◦◦◦◦———

W HEN arriving at a hotel, escort your companion to the parlour, and leave her there whilst you engage rooms. As soon as her room is ready, escort her to the door, and leave her, as she will probably wish to change her dress or lie down, after the fatigue of travelling. If you remain chatting in the parlour, although she may be too polite to give any sign of weariness, you may feel sure she is longing to go to a room where she can bathe her face and smooth her hair.

———◦◦◦◦———

I F you remain in the hotel to any meal, ask before you leave her, at what hour she wishes to dine, sup, or breakfast, and at that hour, knock at her door, and escort her to the table.

———◦◦◦◦———

I F you remain in the city at which her journey terminates, you should call the day after your arrival upon the companion of your journey. If, previous to that journey, you have never met her, she has the privilege of continuing the acquaintance or not as she pleases, so if all your gallantry is repaid by a cut the next time you meet her, you must submit, and hope for better luck next time. In such a case, you are at liberty to decline escorting her again should the request be made.

WHEN travelling alone, your opportunities to display your gallantry will be still more numerous. To offer to carry a bag for a lady who is unattended, to raise or lower a window for her, offer to check her baggage, procure her a hack, give her your arm from car to boat or boat to car, assist her children over the bad crossings, or in fact extend any such kindness, will mark you as a gentleman, and win you the thanks due to your courtesy. Be careful however not to be too attentive, as you then become officious, and embarrass when you mean to please.

IF you are going to travel in other countries, in Europe, especially, I would advise you to study the languages, before you attempt to go abroad. French is the tongue you will find most useful in Europe, as it is spoken in the courts, and amongst diplomatists; but, in order fully to enjoy a visit to any country, you must speak the language of that country. You can then visit in the private houses, see life among the peasantry, go with confidence from village to town, from city to city, learning more of the country in one day from familiar intercourse with the natives, than you would learn in a year from guidebooks or the explanations of your courier. The way to really enjoy a journey through a strange land, is not to roll over the high ways in your carriage, stop at the hotels, and be led to the points of interest by your guide, but to shoulder your knapsack, or take up your valise, and make a pedestrian tour through the hamlets and villages.

———◦◦◦◦———

TAKE a room at a hotel in the principal cities if you will, and see all that your guide book commands you to seek, and then start on your own tour of investigation, and believe me you will enjoy your independent walks and chats with the villagers and peasants, infinitely more than your visits dictated by others. Of course, to enjoy this mode of travelling, you must have some knowledge of the language, and if you start with only a very slight acquaintance with it, you will be surprised to find how rapidly you will acquire the power to converse, when you are thus forced to speak in that language, or be entirely silent.

———◦◦◦◦———

YOUR pocket, too, will be the gainer by the power to arrange your own affairs. If you travel with a courier and depend upon him to arrange your hotel bills and other matters, you will be cheated by everyone, from the boy who blacks your boots, to the magnificent artist, who undertakes to fill your picture gallery with the works of the 'old masters'. If Murillo, Raphael, and Guido could see the pictures brought annually to this country as genuine works of their pencils, we are certain that they would tear their ghostly hair, wring their shadowy hands, and return to the tomb again in disgust. Ignorant of the language of the country you are visiting, you will be swindled in the little villages and the large cities by the innkeepers and the hack-drivers, in the country and in the town, morning, noon, and evening, daily, hourly, and weekly; so, again I say, study the languages if you propose going abroad.

I~N~ a foreign country nothing stamps the difference between the gentleman and the clown more strongly than the regard they pay to foreign customs. While the latter will exclaim against every strange dress or dish, and even show signs of disgust if the latter does not please him, the former will endeavour, as far as is in his power, to 'do in Rome as Romans do'.

A~CCUSTOM~ yourself, as soon as possible, to the customs of the nation which you are visiting, and, as far as you can without any violation of principle, follow them. You will add much to your own comfort by so doing, for, as you cannot expect the whole nation to conform to your habits, the sooner you fall in with theirs the sooner you will feel at home in the strange land.

N~EVER~ ridicule or blame any usage which seems to you ludicrous or wrong. You may wound those around you, or you may anger them, and it cannot add to the pleasure of your visit to make yourself unpopular. If in Germany they serve your meat upon marmalade, or your beef raw, or in Italy give you peas in their pods, or in France offer you frog's legs and horsesteaks, if you cannot eat the strange viands, make no remarks and repress every look or gesture of disgust. Try to adapt your taste to the dishes, and if you find that impossible, remove those articles you cannot eat from your plate, and make your meal upon the others, but do this silently and quietly, endeavouring not to attract attention.

———◦◦◦◦———

T HE best travellers are those who can eat cats in China, oil in Greenland, frogs in France, and macaroni in Italy; who can smoke a meerschaum in Germany, ride an elephant in India, shoot partridges in England, and wear a turban in Turkey; in short, in every nation adapt their habits, costume, and taste to the national manners, dress and dishes.

———◦◦◦◦———

D O not, when abroad, speak continually in praise of your own country, or disparagingly of others. If you find others are interested in gaining information about America, speak candidly and freely of its customs, scenery, or products, but not in a way that will imply a contempt of other countries. To turn up your nose at the Thames because the Mississippi is longer and wider, or to sneer at *any* object because you have seen its superior at home, is rude, ill-bred, and in excessively bad taste.

———◦◦◦◦———

Y OU will, of course, meet with much to disapprove, much that will excite your laughter; but control the one and keep silence about the other. If you find fault, do so gently and quietly; if you praise, do so without qualification, sincerely and warmly.

S TUDY well the geography of any country which you may visit, and, as far as possible, its history also. You cannot feel much interest in localities or monuments connected with history, if you are unacquainted with the events which make them worthy of note.

C ONVERSE with any who seem disposed to form an acquaintance. You may thus pass an hour or two pleasantly, obtain useful information, and you need not carry on the acquaintance unless you choose to do so. Amongst the higher circles in Europe you will find many of the customs of each nation in other nations, but it is among the peasants and the people that you find the true nationality.

Y OU may carry with you one rule into every country, which is, that, however much the inhabitants may object to your dress, language, or habits, they will cheerfully acknowledge that the American stranger is perfectly amiable and polite.

CHAPTER X

One Hundred Hints
for Gentlemanly Deportment

1. Always avoid any rude or boisterous action, especially when in the presence of ladies. It is not necessary to be stiff, indolent, or sullenly silent, neither is perfect gravity always required, but if you jest let it be with quiet, gentlemanly wit, never depending upon clownish gestures for the effect of a story. Nothing marks the gentleman so soon and so decidedly as quiet, refined ease of manner.

2. Never allow a lady to get a chair for herself, ring a bell, pick up a handkerchief or glove she may have dropped, or, in short, perform any service for herself which you can perform for her, when you are in the room. By extending such courtesies to your mother, sisters, or other members of your family, they become habitual, and are thus more gracefully performed when abroad.

3. Never perform any little service for another with a formal bow or manner as if conferring a favour, but with a quiet gentlemanly ease as if it were, not a ceremonious, unaccustomed performance, but a matter of course, for you to be courteous.

———⸎———

4. It is not necessary to tell *all* that you know; that were mere folly; but what a man says must be what he believes himself, else he violates the first rule for a gentleman's speech – Truth.

———⸎———

5. Avoid gambling as you would poison. Every bet made, even in the most finished circles of society, is a species of gambling, and this ruinous crime comes on by slow degrees. Whilst a man is minding his business, he is playing the best game, and he is sure to win. You will be tempted to the vice by those whom the world calls gentlemen, but you will find that loss makes you angry, and an angry man is never a courteous one; gain excites you to continue the pursuit of the vice; and, in the end you will lose money, good name, health, good conscience, light heart, and honesty; while you gain evil associates, irregular hours and habits, a suspicious, fretful temper, and a remorseful, tormenting conscience. Someone *must* lose in the game; and, if you win it, it is at the risk of driving a fellow creature to despair.

———⸎———

6. Cultivate tact! In society it will be an invaluable aid. Talent is something, but tact is everything. Talent is serious, sober,

grave, and respectable; tact is all that and more too. It is not a sixth sense, but it is the life of all the five. It is the *open* eye, the *quick* ear, the *judging* taste, the *keen* smell, and the *lively* touch; it is the interpreter of all riddles – the surmounter of all difficulties – the remover of all obstacles. It is useful in all places, and at all times; it is useful in solitude, for it shows a man his way *into* the world; it is useful in society, for it shows him his way *through* the world. Talent is power – tact is skill; talent is weight – tact is momentum; talent knows what to do – tact knows how to do it; talent makes a man respectable – tact will make him respected; talent is wealth – tact is ready money. For all the practical purposes of society tact carries against talent ten to one.

7. Nature has left every man a capacity of being agreeable, though all cannot *shine* in company; but there are many men sufficiently qualified for both, who, by a very few faults, that a little attention would soon correct, are not so much as tolerable. Watch, avoid such faults.

8. Habits of self-possession and self-control acquired early in life, are the best foundation for the formation of gentlemanly manners. If you unite with this the constant intercourse with ladies and gentlemen of refinement and education, you will add to the dignity of perfect self-command, the polished ease of polite society.

9. Avoid a conceited manner. It is exceedingly ill-bred to assume a manner as if you were superior to those around you, and it is, too, a proof, not of superiority but of vulgarity. And to avoid this manner, avoid the foundation of it, and cultivate humility. The praises of others should be of use to you, in teaching, not what you are, perhaps, but in pointing out what you ought to be.

---

10. Avoid pride, too; it often miscalculates, and more often misconceives. The proud man places himself at a distance from other men; seen through that distance, others, perhaps, appear little to him; but he forgets that this very distance causes him also to appear little to others.

---

11. A gentleman's title suggests to him humility and affability; to be easy of access, to pass by neglects and offences, especially from inferiors; neither to despise any for their bad fortune or misery, nor to be afraid to own those who are unjustly oppressed; not to domineer over inferiors, nor to be either disrespectful or cringing to superiors; not standing upon his family name, or wealth, but making these secondary to his attainments in civility, industry, gentleness, and discretion.

---

12. Chesterfield says, 'All ceremonies are, in themselves, very silly things; but yet a man of the world should know them. They are the outworks of manners, which would be too often broken in upon if it were not for that defence which keeps the enemy at a proper distance. It is for that reason I always treat

fools and coxcombs with great ceremony, true good breeding not being a sufficient barrier against them.'

———∘◦◯◦∘———

13. When you meet a lady at the foot of a flight of stairs, do not wait for her to ascend, but bow, and go up before her.

———∘◦◯◦∘———

14. In meeting a lady at the head of a flight of stairs, wait for her to precede you in the descent.

———∘◦◯◦∘———

15. Avoid slang. It does not beautify, but it sullies conversation. Just listen, for a moment, to our fast young man, or the ape of a fast young man, who thinks that to be a man he must speak in the dark phraseology of slang. If he does anything on his own responsibility, he does it on his own 'hook'. If he sees anything remarkably good, he calls it a 'stunner', the superlative of which is a 'regular stunner'. If a man is requested to pay a tavern bill, he is asked if he will 'stand Sam'. If he meets a savage-looking dog, he calls him an 'ugly customer'. If he meets an eccentric man, he calls him a 'rummy old cove'. A sensible man is a 'chap that is up to snuff'. Our young friend never scolds, but 'blows up'; never pays, but 'stumps up'; never finds it too difficult to pay, but is 'hard up'.

———∘◦◯◦∘———

16. There are few traits of social life more repulsive than tyranny. I refer not to the wrongs, real or imaginary, that

engage our attention in ancient and modern history; my tyrants are not those who have waded through blood to thrones, and grievously oppress their brother men. I speak of the *petty* tyrants of the fireside and the social circle, who trample like very despots on the opinions of their fellows. You meet people of this class everywhere; they stalk by your side in the streets; they seat themselves in the pleasant circle on the hearth, casting a gloom on gaiety; and they start up dark and scowling in the midst of scenes of innocent mirth, to chill and frown down every participator. They 'pooh! pooh!' at every opinion advanced; they make the lives of their mothers, sisters, wives, children, unbearable. Beware then of tyranny. A gentleman is ever humble, and the tyrant is never courteous.

17. Cultivate the virtues of the soul, strong principle, incorruptible integrity, usefulness, refined intellect, and fidelity in seeking for truth. A man in proportion as he has these virtues will be honoured and welcomed everywhere.

18. Gentility is neither in birth, wealth, or fashion, but in the mind. A high sense of honour, a determination never to take a mean advantage of another, adherence to truth, delicacy and politeness towards those with whom we hold intercourse, are the essential characteristics of a gentleman.

19. Little attentions to your mother, your wife, and your sister, will beget much love. The man who is a rude husband, son,

and brother, cannot be a gentleman; he may ape the manners of one, but, wanting the refinement of heart that would make him courteous at home, his politeness is but a thin cloak to cover a rude, unpolished mind.

---

20. At table, always eat slowly, but do not delay those around you by toying with your food, or neglecting the business before you to chat, till all the others are ready to leave the table, but must wait until you repair your negligence, by hastily swallowing your food.

---

21. Are you a husband? Custom entitles you to be the 'lord and master' over your household. But don't assume the *master* and sink the *lord*. Remember that noble generosity, forbearance, amiability, and integrity are the *lordly* attributes of man. As a husband, therefore, exhibit the true nobility of man, and seek to govern your household by the display of high moral excellence.

---

22. Perhaps the true definition of a gentleman is this: 'Whoever is open, loyal, and true; whoever is of humane and affable demeanour; whoever is honourable in himself, and in his judgement of others, and requires no law but his word to make him fulfil an engagement; such a man is a gentleman, be he in the highest or lowest rank of life, a man of elegant refinement and intellect, or the most unpolished tiller of the ground.'

23. In the street, etiquette does not require a gentleman to take off his glove to shake hands with a lady, unless her hand is uncovered. In the house, however, the rule is imperative, he must not offer a lady a gloved hand. In the street, if his hand be very warm or very cold, or the glove cannot be readily removed, it is much better to offer the covered hand than to offend the lady's touch, or delay the salutation during an awkward fumble to remove the glove.

24. Sterne says, 'True courtship consists in a number of quiet, gentlemanly attentions, not so pointed as to alarm, not so vague as to be misunderstood.' A clown will terrify by his boldness, a proud man chill by his reserve, but a gentleman will win by the happy mixture of the two.

25. Use no profane language, utter no word that will cause the most virtuous to blush. Profanity is a mark of low breeding; and the tendency of using indecent and profane language is degrading to your minds. Its injurious effects may not be felt at the moment, but they will continue to manifest themselves to you through life. They may never be obliterated; and, if you allow the fault to become habitual, you will often find at your tongue's end some expressions which you would not use for any money. By being careful on this point you may save yourself much mortification and sorrow.

26. Courteous and friendly conduct may, probably will, sometimes meet with an unworthy and ungrateful return; but the absence of gratitude and similar courtesy on the part of the receiver cannot destroy the self-approbation which recompenses the giver. We may scatter the seeds of courtesy and kindness around us at little expense. Some of them will inevitably fall on good ground, and grow up into benevolence in the minds of others, and all of them will bear the fruit of happiness in the bosom whence they spring. A kindly action always fixes itself on the heart of the truly thoughtful and polite man.

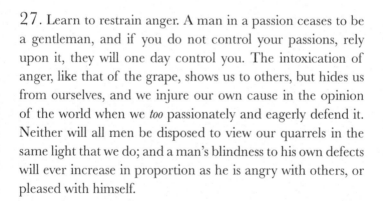

27. Learn to restrain anger. A man in a passion ceases to be a gentleman, and if you do not control your passions, rely upon it, they will one day control you. The intoxication of anger, like that of the grape, shows us to others, but hides us from ourselves, and we injure our own cause in the opinion of the world when we *too* passionately and eagerly defend it. Neither will all men be disposed to view our quarrels in the same light that we do; and a man's blindness to his own defects will ever increase in proportion as he is angry with others, or pleased with himself.

28. Keep good company or none. You will lose your own self-respect, and habits of courtesy sooner and more effectually by intercourse with low company, than in any other manner; while, in good company, these virtues will be cultivated and become habitual.

29. Keep your engagements. Nothing is ruder than to make an engagement, be it of business or pleasure, and break it. If your memory is not sufficiently retentive to keep all the engagements you make stored within it, carry a little memorandum book and enter them there. Especially, keep any appointment made with a lady, for, depend upon it, the fair sex forgive any other fault in good breeding, sooner than a broken engagement.

30. Avoid personality; nothing is more ungentlemanly. The tone of good company is marked by its entire absence. Among well-informed persons there are plenty of topics to discuss, without giving pain to anyone present.

31. Make it a rule to be always punctual in keeping an appointment, and, when it is convenient, be a little beforehand. Such a habit ensures that composure and ease which is the very essence of gentlemanly deportment; want of it keeps you always in a fever and bustle and no man who is hurried and feverish appears so well as he whose punctuality keeps him cool and composed.

32. It is right to cultivate a laudable ambition, but do not exaggerate your capacity. The world will not give you credit for half what you esteem yourself. Some men think it so much

gained to pass for more than they are worth; but in most cases the deception will be discovered, sooner or later, and the rebound will be greater than the gain. We may, therefore, set it down as a truth, that it is a damage to a man to have credit for greater powers than he possesses.

33. Be ready to apologise when you have committed a fault which gives offence. Better, far better, to retain a friend by a frank, courteous apology for offence given, than to make an enemy by obstinately denying or persisting in the fault.

34. An apology made to yourself must be accepted. No matter how great the offence, a gentleman cannot keep his anger after an apology has been made, and thus, amongst truly well-bred men, an apology is always accepted.

35. Unless you have something of real importance to ask or communicate, do not stop a gentleman in the street during business hours. You may detain him from important engagements, and, though he may be too well-bred to show annoyance, he will not thank you for such detention.

36. If, when on your way to fulfil an engagement, a friend stops you in the street, you may, without committing any breach of etiquette, tell him of your appointment, and release

yourself from a long talk, but do so in a courteous manner, expressing regret for the necessity.

---

37. If, when meeting two gentlemen, you are obliged to detain one of them, apologise to the other for so doing, whether he is an acquaintance or a stranger, and do not keep him waiting a moment longer than is necessary.

---

38. Have you a sister? Then love and cherish her with all that pure and holy friendship which renders a brother so worthy and noble. Learn to appreciate her sweet influence as portrayed in the following words:

'He who has never known a sister's kind administration, nor felt his heart warming beneath her endearing smile and love-beaming eye, has been unfortunate indeed. It is not to be wondered at if the fountains of pure feeling flow in his bosom but sluggishly, or if the gentle emotions of his nature be lost in the sterner attributes of mankind.

'"That man has grown up among affectionate sisters," I once heard a lady of much observation and experience remark.

'"And why do you think so?" said I.

'"Because of the rich development of all the tender feelings of the heart."'

---

39. When walking with a friend in the street, never leave him to speak to another friend without apologising for so doing.

---

40. If walking with a lady, never leave her alone in the street, under any circumstances. It is a gross violation of etiquette to do so.

---

41. The most truly gentlemanly man is he who is the most unselfish, so I would say in the words of the Rev. J. A. James:

'Live for some purpose in the world. Act your part well. Fill up the measure of duty to others. Conduct yourselves so that you shall be missed with sorrow when you are gone. Multitudes of our species are living in such a selfish manner that they are not likely to be remembered after their disappearance. They leave behind them scarcely any traces of their existence, but are forgotten almost as though they had never been. They are while they live, like one pebble lying unobserved amongst a million on the shore; and when they die, they are like that same pebble thrown into the sea, which just ruffles the surface, sinks, and is forgotten, without being missed from the beach. They are neither regretted by the rich, wanted by the poor, nor celebrated by the learned. Who has been the better for their life? Who has been the worse for their death? Whose tears have they dried up? whose wants supplied? whose miseries have they healed? Who would unbar the gate of life, to re-admit them to existence? or what face would greet them back again to our world with a smile? Wretched, unproductive mode of existence! Selfishness is its own curse; it is a starving vice. The man who does no good, gets none. He is like the heath in the desert, neither yielding fruit, nor seeing when good cometh – a stunted, dwarfish, miserable shrub.'

42. Separate the syllables of the word gentleman, and you will see that the first requisite must be gentleness – *gentle*-man. Mackenzie says, 'Few persons are sufficiently aware of the power of gentleness. It is slow in working, but it is infallible in its results. It makes no noise; it neither invites attention, nor provokes resistance; but it is God's great law, in the moral as in the natural world, for accomplishing great results. The progressive dawn of day, the flow of the tide, the lapse of time, the changes of the seasons – these are carried on by slow and imperceptible degrees, yet their progress and issue none can mistake or resist. Equally certain and surprising are the triumphs of gentleness. It assumes nothing, yet it can disarm the stoutest opposition; it yields, but yielding is the element of its strength; it endures, but in the warfare victory is not gained by doing, but by suffering.'

43. Perfect composure of manner requires perfect peace of mind, so you should, as far as lies in human power, avoid the evils which make an unquiet mind, and, first of all, avoid that cheating, swindling process called 'running in debt'. Owe no man anything; avoid it as you would avoid war, pestilence, and famine. Hate it with a perfect hatred. As you value comfort,

quiet, and independence, keep out of debt. As you value a healthy appetite, placid temper, pleasant dreams, and happy wakings, keep out of debt. It is the hardest of all task-masters; the most cruel of all oppressors. It is a millstone about the neck. It is an incubus on the heart. It furrows the forehead with premature wrinkles. It drags the nobleness and kindness out of the port and bearing of a man; it takes the soul out of his laugh, and all stateliness and freedom from his walk. Come not, then, under its crushing dominion.

44. Speak gently; a kind refusal will often wound less than a rough, ungracious assent.

45. 'In private, watch your thoughts; in your family, watch your temper; in society, watch your tongue.'

46. The true secret of pleasing all the world, is to have an humble opinion of yourself. True goodness is invariably accompanied by gentleness, courtesy, and humility. Those people who are always 'sticking on their dignity', are continually losing friends, making enemies, and fostering a spirit of unhappiness in themselves.

47. Are you a merchant? Remember that the counting-house is no less a school of manners and temper than a school of

morals. Vulgarity, imperiousness, peevishness, caprice on the part of the heads, will produce their corresponding effects upon the household. Some merchants are petty tyrants. Some are too surly to be fit for any charge, unless it be that of taming a shrew. The coarseness of others, in manner and language, must either disgust or contaminate all their subordinates. These are sad infirmities. Men ought not to have clerks until they know how to treat them. Their own comfort, too, would be greatly enhanced by a different deportment.

48. If you are about to enter, or leave, a store or any door, and unexpectedly meet a lady going the other way, stand aside and raise your hat whilst she passes. If she is going the same way, and the door is closed, pass before her, saying, 'allow me', or, 'permit me', – open the door, and hold it open whilst she passes.

49. In entering a room where you will meet ladies, take your hat, cane, and gloves in your left hand, that your right may be free to offer to them.

50. Never offer to shake hands with a lady; she will, if she wishes you to do so, offer her hand to you, and it is an impertinence for you to do so first.

51. If you are seated in the most comfortable chair in a public room, and a lady, an invalid, or an old man enters, rise, and offer your seat, even if they are strangers to you. Many men will attend to these civilities when with friends or acquaintances, and neglect them amongst strangers, but the true gentleman will not wait for an introduction before performing an act of courtesy.

---

52. As both flattery and slander are in the highest degree blameable and ungentlemanly, I would quote the rule of Bishop Beveridge, which effectually prevents both. He says, 'Never speak of a man's virtue before his face, nor of his faults behind his back.'

---

53. Never enter a room, in which there are ladies, after smoking, until you have purified both your mouth, teeth, hair, and clothes. If you wish to smoke just before entering a saloon, wear an old coat and carefully brush your hair and teeth before resuming your own.

---

54. Never endeavour to attract the attention of a friend by nudging him, touching his foot or hand secretly, or making him a gesture. If you cannot speak to him frankly, you had best let him alone; for these signals are generally made with the intention of ridiculing a third person, and that is the height of rudeness.

55. Button-holding is a common but most blameable breach of good manners. If a man requires to be forcibly detained to listen to you, you are as rude in thus detaining him, as if you had put a pistol to his head and threatened to blow his brains out if he stirred.

56. It is a great piece of rudeness to make a remark in general company, which is intelligible to one person only. To call out, 'George, I met D.L. yesterday, and he says he will attend to that matter,' is as bad as if you went to George and whispered in his ear.

57. In your intercourse with servants, nothing will mark you as a well-bred man, so much as a gentle, courteous manner. A request will make your wishes attended to as quickly as a command, and thanks for a service, oil the springs of the servant's labour immensely. Rough, harsh commands may make your orders obeyed well and promptly, but they will be executed unwillingly, in fear, and, probably, dislike, while courtesy and kindness will win a willing spirit as well as prompt service.

58. Avoid eccentric conduct. It does not, as many suppose, mark a man of genius. Most men of true genius are gentlemanly and reserved in their intercourse with other men, and there are many fools whose folly is called eccentricity.

59. Avoid familiarity. Neither treat others with too great cordiality nor suffer them to take liberties with you. To check the familiarity of others, you need not become stiff, sullen, nor cold, but you will find that excessive politeness on your own part, sometimes with a little formality, will soon abash the intruder.

60. Lazy, lounging attitudes in the presence of ladies are very rude.

61. It is only the most arrant coxcomb who will boast of the favour shown him by a lady, speak of her by her first name, or allow others to jest with him upon his friendship or admiration for her. If he really admires her, and has reason to hope for a future engagement with her, her name should be as sacred to him as if she were already his wife; if, on the contrary, he is not on intimate terms with her, then he adds a lie to his excessively bad breeding, when using her name familiarly.

62. 'He that can please nobody is not so much to be pitied as he that nobody can please.'

63. Speak without obscurity or affectation. The first is a mark of pedantry, the second a sign of folly. A wise man will speak always clearly and intelligibly.

---

64. To betray a confidence is to make yourself despicable. Many things are said among friends which are not said under a seal of secrecy, but are understood to be confidential, and a truly honourable man will never violate this tacit confidence. It is really as sacred as if the most solemn promises of silence bound your tongue; more so, indeed, to the true gentleman, as his sense of honour, not his word, binds him.

---

65. Chesterfield says, 'As learning, honour, and virtue are absolutely necessary to gain you the esteem and admiration of mankind, politeness and good breeding are equally necessary to make you welcome and agreeable in conversation and common life. Great talents, such as honour, virtue, learning, and parts are above the generality of the world, who neither possess them themselves nor judge of them rightly in others; but all people are judges of the lesser talents, such as civility, affability, and an obliging, agreeable address and manner; because they feel the good effects of them, as making society easy and pleasing.'

---

66. 'Good sense must, in many cases, determine good breeding; because the same thing that would be civil at one time and to one person, may be quite otherwise at another time and to another person.'

67. Nothing can be more ill-bred than to meet a polite remark addressed to you, either with inattention or a rude answer.

68. Spirit is now a very fashionable word, but it is terribly misapplied. In the present day to act with spirit and speak with spirit means to act rashly and speak indiscreetly. A gentleman shows his spirit by firm, but gentle words and resolute actions. He is spirited but neither rash nor timid.

69. 'Use kind words. They do not cost much. It does not take long to utter them. They never blister the tongue or lips in their passage into the world, or occasion any other kind of bodily suffering. And we have never heard of any mental trouble arising from this quarter.

'Kind words make other people good-natured. Cold words freeze people, and hot words scorch them, and sarcastic words irritate them, and bitter words make them bitter, and wrathful words make them wrathful. And kind words also produce their own image on men's souls. And a beautiful image it is. They soothe, and quiet, and comfort the hearer. They shame him out of his sour, morose, unkind feelings, and he has to become kind himself.'

70. The first step towards pleasing everyone is to endeavour to offend no one. To give pain by a light or jesting remark is as much a breach of etiquette, as to give pain by a wound made with a steel weapon, is a breach of humanity.

---

71. 'A gentleman will never use his tongue to rail and brawl against anyone; to speak evil of others in their absence; to exaggerate any of his statements; to speak harshly to children or to the poor; to swear, lie, or use improper language; to hazard random and improbable statements; to speak rashly or violently upon any subject; to deceive people by circulating false reports, or to offer up *lip*-service in religion. But he will use it to convey to mankind useful information; to instruct his family and others who need it; to warn and reprove the wicked; to comfort and console the afflicted; to cheer the timid and fearful; to defend the innocent and oppressed; to plead for the widow and orphan; to congratulate the success of the virtuous, and to confess, tearfully and prayerfully, his faults.'

---

72. Chesterfield says, 'Civility is particularly due to all women; and, remember, that no provocation whatsoever can justify any man in not being civil to every woman; and the greatest man would justly be reckoned a brute if he were not civil to the meanest woman. It is due to their sex, and is the only protection they have against the superior strength of ours; nay, even a little is allowable with women: and a man may, without weakness, tell a women she is either handsomer or wiser than she is.' (Chesterfield would not have said this in the present age of strong-minded, sensible women.)

73. There is much tact and good breeding to be displayed in the correction of any little error that may occur in conversation. To say, shortly, – 'You are wrong! I know better!' is rude, and your friends will much more readily admit an error if you say courteously and gently, 'Pardon me, but I must take the liberty of correcting you,' or, 'You will allow me, I am sure, to tell you that your informant made an error.' If such an error is of no real importance, it is better to let it pass unnoticed.

74. Intimate friends and relations should be careful when they go out into the world together, or admit others to their own circle, that they do not make a bad use of the knowledge which they have gained of each other by their intimacy. Nothing is more common than this; and, did it not mostly proceed from mere carelessness, it would be superlatively ungenerous. You seldom need wait for the written life of a man to hear about his weaknesses, or what are supposed to be such, if you know his intimate friends, or meet him in company with them.

75. In making your first visit anywhere, you will be less apt to offend by being too ceremonious, than by being too familiar.

76. With your friends remember the old proverb, that, 'Familiarity breeds contempt.'

77. If you meet, in society, with anyone, be it a gentleman or a lady, whose timidity or bashfulness, shows them unaccustomed to meeting others, endeavour, by your own gentleness and courtesy, to place them more at ease, and introduce to them those who will aid you in this endeavour.

78. If, when walking with a gentleman friend, you meet a lady to whom your friend bows, you, too, must touch or raise your hat, though you are not acquainted with the lady.

79. 'Although it is now very much the custom, in many wealthy families, for the butler to remove the dishes from the table and carve them on the sideboard, thus saving trouble to the master or mistress of the house, and time to the guests, the practice is not so general even amongst what are called the higher classes of society that general instructions for carving will be uninteresting to them, to say nothing of the more numerous class, who, although enabled to place good dishes before their friends, are not wealthy enough to keep a butler if they were so inclined. Good carving is, to a certain extent, indicative of good society, for it proves to company that the host does not give a dinner party for the first time, but is accustomed to receive friends, and frequently to dispense the cheer of a hospitable board.'

80. Years may pass over our heads without affording an opportunity for acts of high beneficence or extensive utility; whereas, not a day passes, but in common transactions of life, and, especially in the intercourse of society, courtesy finds place for promoting the happiness of others, and for strengthening in ourselves the habits of unselfish politeness. There are situations, not a few, in human life, when an encouraging reception, a condescending behaviour, and a look of sympathy, bring greater relief to the heart than the most bountiful gift.

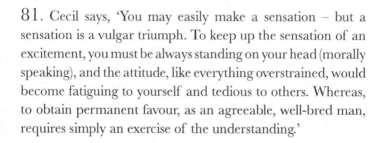

81. Cecil says, 'You may easily make a sensation – but a sensation is a vulgar triumph. To keep up the sensation of an excitement, you must be always standing on your head (morally speaking), and the attitude, like everything overstrained, would become fatiguing to yourself and tedious to others. Whereas, to obtain permanent favour, as an agreeable, well-bred man, requires simply an exercise of the understanding.'

82. There is no vice more truly ungentlemanly than that of using profane language. Lamont says: 'Whatever fortune may be made by perjury, I believe there never was a man who made a fortune by common swearing. It often appears that men pay for swearing, but it seldom happens that they are paid for it. It is not easy to perceive what honour or credit is connected with it. Does any man receive promotion because he is a notable blusterer? Or is any man advanced to dignity because he is expert at profane swearing? Never. Low must be the character which such impertinence will exalt: high must

be the character which such impertinence will not degrade. Inexcusable, therefore, must be the practice which has neither reason nor passion to support it.'

—⚬❀⚬—

83. Dr Johnson says that to converse well 'there must, in the first place, be knowledge – there must be materials; in the second place, there must be a command of words; in the third place, there must be imagination to place things in such views as they are not commonly seen in; and, in the fourth place, there must be a presence of mind, and a resolution that is not to be overcome by failure – this last is an essential requisite; for want of it, many people do not excel in conversation.'

—⚬❀⚬—

84. 'Do not constantly endeavour to draw the attention of all upon yourself when in company. Leave room for your hearers to imagine something within you beyond what you speak; and, remember, the more you are praised the more you will be envied.'

—⚬❀⚬—

85. Be very careful to treat with attention and respect those who have lately met with misfortunes, or have suffered from loss of fortune. Such persons are apt to think themselves slighted, when no such thing is intended. Their minds, being already sore, feel the least rub very severely, and who would thus cruelly add affliction to the afflicted? Not the *gentleman* certainly.

—⚬❀⚬—

86. There is hardly any bodily blemish which a winning behaviour will not conceal or make tolerable; and there is no external grace which ill nature or affectation will not deform.

87. Good humour is the only shield to keep off the darts of the satirist; but if you are the first to laugh at a jest made upon yourself, others will laugh *with* you instead of *at* you.

88. Whenever you see a person insult his inferiors, you may feel assured that he is the man who will be servile and cringing to his superiors; and he who acts the bully to the weak, will play the coward when with the strong.

89. Maintain, in every word, a strict regard for perfect truth. Do not think of one falsity as harmless, another as slight, a third as unintended. Cast them all aside. They may be light and accidental, but they are an ugly soot from the smoke of the pit for all that, and it is better to have your heart swept clean of them, without stopping to consider whether they are large and black.

90. The advantage and necessity of cheerfulness and intelligent intercourse with the world is strongly to be recommended. A man who keeps aloof from society and lives only for himself, does not fulfil the wise intentions of

Providence, who designed that we should be a mutual help and comfort to each other in life.

---

91. Chesterfield says, 'Merit and good breeding will make their way everywhere. Knowledge will introduce man, and good breeding will endear him to the best companies; for, politeness and good breeding are absolutely necessary to adorn any, or all, other good qualities or talents. Without them, no knowledge, no perfection whatever, is seen in its best light. The scholar, without good breeding, is a pedant; the philosopher, a cynic; the soldier, a brute; and every man disagreeable.'

---

92. It is very seldom that a man may permit himself to tell stories in society; they are, generally, tedious, and, to many present, will probably have all the weariness of a 'twice-told tale'. A short, brilliant anecdote, which is especially applicable to the conversation going on, is all that a well-bred man will ever permit himself to inflict.

---

93. It is better to take the tone of the society into which you are thrown, than to endeavour to lead others after you. The way to become truly popular is to be grave with the grave, jest with the gay, and converse sensibly with those who seek to display their sense.

---

94. Watch each of your actions, when in society, that all the habits which you contract there may be useful and good ones. Like flakes of snow that fall unperceived upon the earth, the seemingly unimportant events of life succeed one another. As the snow gathers together, so are our habits formed. No single flake that is added to the pile produces a sensible change – no single action creates, however it may exhibit, a man's character; but, as the tempest hurls the avalanche down the mountain, and overwhelms the inhabitant and his habitation, so passion, acting upon the elements of mischief, which pernicious habits have brought together by imperceptible accumulation, may overthrow the edifice of truth and virtue.

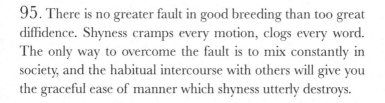

95. There is no greater fault in good breeding than too great diffidence. Shyness cramps every motion, clogs every word. The only way to overcome the fault is to mix constantly in society, and the habitual intercourse with others will give you the graceful ease of manner which shyness utterly destroys.

96. If you are obliged to leave a large company at an early hour, take French leave. Slip away unperceived, if you can, but, at any rate, without any formal leave-taking.

97. Avoid quarrels. If you are convinced, even, that you have the right side in an argument, yield your opinion gracefully, if this is the only way to avoid a quarrel, saying, 'We cannot agree, I see, but this inability must not deprive me of a friend,

so we will discuss the subject no further.' Few men will be able to resist your courtesy and good nature, but many would try to combat an obstinate adherence to your own side of the question.

---

98. Avoid the filthy habit of which foreigners in this country so justly complain – I mean spitting.

---

99. If anyone bows to you in the street, return the bow. It may be an acquaintance whose face you do not immediately recognise, and if it is a stranger who mistakes you for another, your courteous bow will relieve him from the embarrassment arising from his mistake.

---

100. 'Conversation may be carried on successfully by persons who have no idea that it is or may be an art, as clever things are sometimes done without study. But there can be no certainty of good conversation in ordinary circumstances, and amongst ordinary minds, unless certain rules be observed, and certain errors be avoided.'

'THE first and greatest rule unquestionably is, that all must be favourably disposed towards each other, and willing to be pleased. There must be no sullen or uneasy-looking person – no one who evidently thinks he has fallen into unsuitable company, and whose sole aim it is to take care lest his dignity be injured – no one whose feelings are of so morose or ascetic a kind that he cannot join without observable pain and hesitation in the playfulness of the scene – no matter-of-fact person, who takes all things literally, and means all things literally, and thinks it as great a crime to say something in jest as to do it in earnest. One of any of these classes of persons is sufficient to mar the enjoyments of a hundred. The matter-of-factish may do very well with the matter-of-factish, the morose with the morose, the stilted with the stilted; and they should accordingly keep amongst themselves respectively. But, for what is generally recognised as agreeable conversation, minds exempted from these peculiarities are required.'

CHAPTER XI

Parties

Now, there are many different kinds of parties. There are the evening party, the matinee, the reading, dancing, and singing parties, the picnic, the boating, and the riding parties; and the duties for each one are distinct, yet, in many points, similar. Our present subject is:

THE EVENING PARTY

These are of two kinds, large and small. For the first, you will receive a formal card, containing the compliments of your hostess for a certain evening, and this calls for full dress, a dress coat, and white or very light gloves. To the small party you will probably be invited verbally, or by a more familiar style of note than the compliment card. Here you may wear gloves if you will, but you need not do so unless perfectly agreeable to yourself.

If you are to act as escort to a lady, you must call at the hour she chooses to name, and the most elegant way is to take a carriage for her. If you wish to present a bouquet, you may do so with perfect propriety.

—◦❀◦—

WHEN you reach the house of your hostess for the evening, escort your companion to the dressing room, and leave her at the door. After you have deposited your own hat and great coat in the gentlemen's dressing room, return to the ladies' door and wait for your companion. Offer her your right arm, and lead her to the drawing room, and, at once, to the hostess, then take her to a seat, and remain with her until she has other companions, before you seek any of your own friends in the room.

—◦❀◦—

THERE is much more real enjoyment and sociability in a *well-arranged* party, than in a ball, though many of the points of etiquette to be observed in the latter are equally applicable to the former. There is more time allowed for conversation, and, as there are not so many people collected, there is also more opportunity for forming acquaintances. At a *soirée, par excellence*, music, dancing, and conversation are all admissible, and if the hostess has tact and discretion this variety is very pleasing. As there are many times when there is no pianist or music engaged for dancing, you will do well, if you are a performer on the pianoforte, to learn some quadrilles, and round dances, that you may volunteer your services as *orchestra*. Do not, in this case, wait to be solicited to play, but offer your services to the hostess, or, if there is a lady at the piano, ask permission to relieve her. To turn the leaves for another, and sometimes call figures, are also good-natured and well-bred actions.

—◦❀◦—

T HERE is one piece of rudeness very common at parties, against which I would caution you. Young people very often form a group, and indulge in the most boisterous merriment and loud laughter, for jests known only to themselves. Do not join such a group. A well-bred man, while he is cheerful and gay, will avoid any appearance of romping in society.

I F dancing is to be the amusement for the evening, your first dance should be with the lady whom you accompanied, then, invite your hostess, and, if there are several ladies in the family you must invite each of them once, in the course of the evening. If you go alone, invite the ladies of the house before dancing with any of your other lady friends.

N EVER attempt any dance with which you are not perfectly familiar. Nothing is more awkward and annoying than to have one dancer, by his ignorance of the figures, confuse all the others in the set, and certainly no man wants to show off his ignorance of the steps of a round dance before a room full of company.

D O not devote yourself too much to one lady. A party is meant to promote sociability, and a man who persists in a tête-à-tête for the evening, destroys this intention. Besides you prevent others from enjoying the pleasure of intercourse with the lady you thus monopolise.

———⊸⊙⊚⊙⊶———

Avoid any affectation of great intimacy with any lady present; and even if you really enjoy such intimacy, or she is a relative, do not appear to have confidential conversation, or, in any other way, affect airs of secrecy or great familiarity.

———⊸⊙⊚⊙⊶———

Dance easily and gracefully, keeping perfect time, but not taking too great pains with your steps. If your whole attention is given to your feet or carriage, you will probably be mistaken for a dancing master.

———⊸⊙⊚⊙⊶———

When you conduct your partner to a seat after a dance, you may sit or stand beside her to converse, unless you see that another gentleman is waiting to invite her to dance.

———⊸⊙⊚⊙⊶———

If music is called for and you are able to play or sing, do so when first invited, or, if you refuse then, do not afterwards comply. If you refuse, and then alter your mind you will either be considered a vain coxcomb, who likes to be urged; or some will conclude that you refused at first from mere caprice, for, if you had a good reason for declining, why change your mind?

———⊸⊙⊚⊙⊶———

NEVER offer to turn the leaves of music for anyone playing, unless you can read the notes, for you run the risk of confusing them, by turning too soon or too late.

IF you sing a good second, never sing with a lady unless she herself invites you. Her friends may wish to hear you sing together, when she herself may not wish to sing with one to whose voice and time she is unaccustomed.

DO not start a conversation whilst anyone is either playing or singing, and if another person commences one, speak in a tone that will not prevent others from listening to the music.

IF you play yourself, do not wait for silence in the room before you begin. If you play well, those really fond of music will cease to converse, and listen to you; and those who do not care for it, will not stop talking if you wait upon the piano stool until day dawn.

RELATIVES should avoid each other at a party, as they can enjoy one another's society at home, and it is the constantly changing intercourse, and complete sociability that make a party pleasant.

PRIVATE concerts and amateur theatricals are very often the occasions for evening parties, and make a very pleasant variety on the usual dancing and small talk. An English writer, speaking of them, says: 'Private concerts and amateur theatricals ought to be very good to be successful. Professionals alone should be engaged for the former, none but real amateurs for the latter. Both ought to be, but rarely are, followed by a supper, since they are generally very fatiguing, if not positively trying. In any case, refreshments and ices should be handed between the songs and the acts. Private concerts are often given in the "morning", that is, from two to six p.m.; in the evening their hours are from eight to eleven. The rooms should be arranged in the same manner as for a reception, the guests should be seated, and as music is the avowed object, a general silence preserved while it lasts. Between the songs the conversation ebbs back again, and the party takes the general form of a reception. For private theatricals, however, where there is no special theatre, and where the curtain is hung, as is most common, between the folding-doors, the audience-room must be filled with chairs and benches in rows, and, if possible, the back rows raised higher than the others. These are often removed when the performance is over, and the guests then converse, or, sometimes, even dance. During the acting it is rude to talk, except in a very low tone, and, be it good or bad, you would never think of hissing.'

IF you are alone, and obliged to retire early from an evening party, do not take leave of your hostess, but slip away unperceived.

I F you have escorted a lady, her time must be yours, and she will tell you when she is ready to go. See whether the carriage has arrived before she goes to the dressing room, and return to the parlour to tell her. If the weather was pleasant when you left home, and you walked, ascertain whether it is still pleasant; if not, procure a carriage for your companion. When it is at the door, join her in the drawing room, and offer your arm to lead her to the hostess for leave-taking, making your own parting bow at the same time, then take your companion to the door of the ladies' dressing room, get your own hat and wait in the entry until she comes out.

W HEN you reach your companion's house, do not accept her invitation to enter, but ask permission to call in the morning, or the following evening, and make that call.

CHAPTER XII

Courtesy at Home

THERE are many men in this world, who would be horror-struck if accused of the least breach of etiquette towards their friends and acquaintances abroad, and yet, who will at home utterly disregard the simplest rules of politeness, if such rules interfere in the least with their own selfish gratification. They disregard the pure and holy ties which should make courtesy at home a pleasure as well as a duty. They forget that home has a sweet poetry of its own, created out of the simplest materials, yet, haunting, more or less, the secret recesses of every human heart; it is divided into a thousand separate poems, which should be full of individual interest, little quiet touches of feeling and golden recollections, which, in the heart of a truly noble man, are interwoven with his very being. Common things are, to him, hallowed and made beautiful by the spell of memory and association, owing all their glory to the halo of his own pure, fond affection.

THE man who shows his contempt for these holy ties and associations by pulling off his mask of courtesy as soon as his foot passes his own threshold, is not really a gentleman, but a selfish tyrant, whose true qualities are not courtesy and politeness, but a hypocritical affectation of them, assumed to obtain a footing in society. Avoid such men. Even though you are one of the favoured ones abroad who receive their gentle courtesy, you may rest assured that the heartless egotism which makes them rude and selfish at home, will make their friendship but a name, if circumstances ever put it to the test. Above all, avoid their example.

———◦◉◎◦———

I N what does the home circle consist? First, there are the parents who have watched over your infancy and childhood, and whom you are commanded by the Highest Power to 'honour'. Then the brothers and sisters, the wife who has left her own home and all its tender ties for your sake, and the children who look to you for example, guidance, and instruction.

———◦◉◎◦———

W HO else on the broad earth can lay the same claim to your gentleness and courtesy that they can? If you are rude at home, then is your politeness abroad a mere cloak to conceal a bad, selfish heart.

———◦◉◎◦———

T HE parents who have anxiously watched over your education, have the first right to the fruits of it, and all the *gentleman* should be exerted to repay them for the care they have taken of you since your birth. All the rules of politeness, of generosity, of good nature, patience, and respectful affection should be exerted for your parents. You owe to them a pure, filial love, void of personal interest, which should prompt you to study all their tastes, their likes, and aversions, in order to indulge the one and avoid the other; you owe to them polite attention, deference to all their wishes, and compliance with their requests. Every joy will be doubled to them, if you show a frank pleasure in its course, and no comfort can soothe the grief of a parent so much as the sympathising love of a dutiful son. If they are old, dependent upon you for support, then can you still better prove to them that the tender care they lavished upon you, when you depended upon their love for everything, was not lost, but was good seed sown upon fruitful ground.

———◦⊙◦———

A N eminent writer, in speaking of a man's duties, says: 'Do all in your power to render your parents comfortable and happy; if they are aged and infirm, be with them as often as you can, carry them tokens of your love, and show them that you feel a tender interest in their happiness. Be all to your parents, which you would wish your children to be to you.'

———◦⊙◦———

N EXT, in the home circle, come your brothers and sisters, and here you will find the little courtesies, which, as a gentleman, should be habitual to you, will ensure the love a man should most highly prize, the love of his brother and sister. Next to his filial love, this is the first tie of his life, and should be valued as it deserves.

I f you are the eldest of the family, you may, by your example, influence your brothers to good or evil, and win or alienate the affections of your little sisters. There is scarcely a more enthusiastic affection in the world than that a sister feels for an elder brother. Even though he may not repay the devotion as it deserves, she will generally cherish it, and invest him with the most heroic qualities, while her tender little heart, though it may quiver with the pain of a harsh word or rude action, will still try to find an excuse for 'brother's' want of affection. If you show an interest in the pursuits of the little circle at whose head your age entitles you to stand, you will soon find they all look up to you, seek your advice, crave your sympathy, and follow your example. The eldest son holds a most responsible position. Should death or infirmity deprive him of a father's counsel, he should be prepared to stand forth as the head of the family, and take his father's place towards his mother and the younger children.

E very man should feel, that in the character and dignity of his sisters, his own honour is involved. An insult or affront offered to them, becomes one to him, and he is the person they will look to for protection, and to prevent its repetition. By his own manner to them he can ensure to them the respect or contempt of other men whom they meet when in his society. How can he expect that his friends will treat his sisters with gentleness, respect, and courtesy, if they see him constantly rude, disrespectful, and contemptuous towards them? But, if his own manner is that of affectionate respect, he need not fear for them rudeness from others, while they are under his protection.

A N American writer says: 'Nothing in a family strikes the eye of a visitor with more delight than to see brothers treat their sisters with kindness, civility, attention, and love. On the contrary, nothing is more offensive or speaks worse for the honour of a family, than that coarse, rude, unkind manner which brothers sometimes exhibit.'

'B EWARE how you speak of your sisters. Even gold is tarnished by much handling. If you speak in their praise – of their beauty, learning, manners, wit, or attentions – you will subject them to taunt and ridicule; if you say anything against them, you will bring reproach upon yourself and them too. If you have occasion to speak of them, do it with modesty and few words. Let others do all the praising and yourself enjoy it. If you are separated from them, maintain with them a correspondence. This will do yourself good as well as them. Do not neglect this duty, nor grow remiss in it. Give your friendly advice and seek theirs in return. As they mingle intimately with their sex, they can enlighten your mind respecting many particulars relating to female character, important for you to know; and, on the other hand, you have the same opportunity to do them a similar service. However long or widely separated from them, keep up your fraternal affection and intercourse. It is ominous of evil when a young man forgets his sister.'

'I F you are living at home with them, you may do them a thousand little services, which will cost you nothing but pleasure, and which will greatly add to theirs. If they wish to go out in the evening – to a lecture, concert, a visit, or any other object, – always be happy, if possible, to wait upon them. Consider their situation, and think how you would wish them to treat you if the case were reversed.'

⸻

A YOUNG man once said to an elderly lady, who expressed her regret at his having taken some trouble and denied himself a pleasure to gratify her: 'Madam, I am far away from my mother and sisters now, but when I was at home, my greatest pleasure was to protect them and gratify all their wishes; let me now place you in their stead, and you will not have cause again to feel regret, for you can think "he *must love* to deny himself for one who represents his mother." The old lady afterwards spoke of him as a perfect gentleman, and was contradicted by a younger person who quoted some fault in etiquette committed by the young man in company. "Ah, that may be," said her friend; "but what I call a gentleman, is not the man who performs to the minutest point all the little ceremonies of society, but the one whose *heart* prompts him to be polite at home."'

⸻

I F you have left the first home circle, that comprising your parents, brothers, and sisters, to take up the duties of a husband and father, you must carry to your new home the same politeness I have advised you to exert in the home of your childhood.

Your wife claims your courtesy more now, even, than when you were courting her. She has given up, for your sake, all the freedom and pleasures of her maidenhood, and to you she looks for a love that will replace them all. Can you disappoint that trusting affection? Before your marriage you thought no stretch of courtesy too great, if the result was to afford her pleasure; why, then, not strive to *keep* her love, by the same gentle courtesy you exerted to *win* it?

'A delicate attention to the minute wants and wishes of your wife, will tend, more than anything else, to the promotion of your domestic happiness. It requires no sacrifices, occupies but a small degree of attention, yet is the fertile source of bliss; since it convinces the object of your regard, that, with the duties of a husband, you have united the more punctilious behaviour of a lover. These trivial tokens of regard certainly make much way in the affections of a woman of sense and discernment, who looks not to the value of the gifts she receives, but perceives in their frequency a continued evidence of the existence and ardour of that love on which the superstructure of her happiness has been erected. The strongest attachment will decline, if you receive it with diminished warmth.'

Mrs Thrale gives the following advice, which is worth the consideration of every young man: 'After marriage,' she says, 'when your violence of passion subsides, and a more cool and tranquil affection takes its place, be not hasty to censure as indifferent, or to lament yourself as unhappy; you have lost that only which it is impossible to retain; and it were graceless amidst the pleasures of a prosperous summer, to regret the blossoms of a transient spring. Neither unwarily condemn your bride's insipidity, till you have recollected that no object, however sublime, no sound, however charming, can continue to transport us with delight, when they no longer strike us with novelty. The skill to renovate the powers of pleasing is said, indeed, to be possessed by some women in an eminent degree, but the artifices of maturity are seldom seen to adorn the innocence of youth. You have made your choice and ought to approve it.'

'To be happy, we must always have something in view. Turn, therefore, your attention to her mind, which will daily grow brighter by polishing. Study some easy science together, and acquire a similarity of tastes, while you enjoy a community of pleasures. You will, by this means, have many pursuits in common, and be freed from the necessity of separating to find amusement; endeavour to cement the present union on every side; let your wife never be kept ignorant of your income, your expenses, your friendships, or your aversions; let her know your very faults, but make them amiable by your virtues; consider all concealment as a breach of fidelity; let her never have anything to find out in your character, and remember that from the moment one of the partners turns spy upon the other, they have commenced a state of hostility.'

'SEEK not for happiness in singularity, and dread a refinement of wisdom as a deviation into folly. Listen not to those sages who advise you always to scorn the counsel of a woman, and if you comply with her requests pronounce you to be wife-ridden. Think not any privation, except of positive evil, an excellence; and do not congratulate yourself that your wife is not a learned lady, or is wholly ignorant how to make a pudding. Cooking and learning are both good in their places, and may both be used with advantage. With regard to expense, I can only observe, that the money laid out in the purchase of luxuries is seldom or ever profitably employed. We live in an age when splendid furniture and glittering equipage are grown too common to catch the notice of the meanest spectator; and for the greater ones, they can only regard our wasteful folly with silent contempt or open indignation.'

'THIS may, perhaps, be a displeasing reflection; but the following consideration ought to make amends. The age we live in pays, I think, a peculiar attention to the higher distinctions of wit, knowledge, and virtue, to which we may more safely, more cheaply, and more honourably aspire.'

'THE person of your lady will not grow more pleasing to you; but, pray, let her not suspect that it grows less so. There is no reproof, however pointed, no punishment, however severe, that a woman of spirit will not prefer to neglect; and if she can endure it without complaint, it only proves that she means to make herself amends by the attention of others for the slights of her husband. For this, and for every other reason, it behoves a married man not to let his politeness fail, though his ardour may abate; but to retain, at least, that general civility towards his own lady which he is willing to pay to every other, and not show a wife of eighteen or twenty years old, that every man in company can treat her with more complaisance than he who so often vowed to her eternal fondness.'

'I T is not my opinion that a young woman should be indulged in every wild wish of her gay heart, or giddy head; but contradiction may be softened by domestic kindness, and quiet pleasures substituted in the place of noisy ones. Public amusements, indeed, are not so expensive as is sometimes imagined; but they tend to alienate the minds of married people from each other. A well-chosen society of friends and acquaintances, more eminent for virtue and good sense than for gaiety and splendour, where the conversation of the day may afford comment for the evening, seems the most rational pleasure that can be afforded. That your own superiority should always be seen, but never felt, seems an excellent general rule.'

'I F your wife is disposed towards jealousy of you, let me beseech you be always explicit with her, never mysterious. Be above delighting in her pain in all things.'

A FTER your duty to your wife comes that towards the children whom God lends to you, to fit them to return pure and virtuous to him. This is your task, responsibility, and trust, to be undertaken prayerfully, earnestly, and humbly, as the highest and most sacred duty this life ever can afford you.

———✦———

T HE relationship between parent and child, is one that appears to have been ordained by Providence, to bring the better feelings of mankind and many domestic virtues into active exercise. The implicit confidence with which children, when properly treated, look up to their elders for guidance is not less beautiful than endearing; and no parents can set about the work of guiding aright, in real earnest, without deriving as much good as they impart. The feeling with which this labour of love would be carried forward is, as the poet writes of mercy, twice blessed: 'It blesses him that gives and him that takes.'

———✦———

A ND yet, in daily life and experience, how seldom do we find these views realised! Children, in too many instances, are looked on as anything but a blessing; they are treated as encumbrances, or worse; and the neglect in which they are brought up, renders it almost impossible for them, when they grow older, to know anything properly of moral or social duties. This result we know, in numerous cases, is not wilful, does not arise from ill intentions on the part of parents, but from want of fixed plans and principles. There are hundreds of families in this country whose daily life is nothing better than a daily scramble, where time and place, from getting up in the morning to going to bed at night, are regarded as matters of chance. In such homes as these, where the inmates are willing to do well, but don't know how, a word in season is often welcome. 'Great principles,' we are told, 'are at the bottom of all things; but to apply them to daily life, many little rules, precautions, and insights are needed.'

THE work of training is, in some degree, lightened by the fact that children are very imitative; what they see others do, they will try to do themselves, and if they see none but good examples, good conduct on their part may naturally be looked for. Children are keen observers, and are very ready at drawing conclusions when they see a want of correspondence between profession and practice, in those who have the care of them. At the age of seven, the child's brain has reached its full growth; it seldom becomes larger after that period, and it then contains the germ of all that the man ever accomplishes. Here is an additional reason for laying down the precept: be yourselves what you wish the children to be. When correction is necessary, let it be administered in such a way as to make the child refrain from doing wrong from a desire to do right, not for the sole reason that wrong brings punishment. All experience teaches us that if a good thing is to be obtained, it must be by persevering diligence; and of all good things, the pleasure arising from a well-trained family is one of the greatest. Parents, or educators, have no right to use their children just as whim or prejudice may dictate. Children are smaller links in the great social chain, and bind together in lasting ties many portions which otherwise would be completely disjointed; their joyousness enlivens many a home, and their innocence is a powerful check and antidote to much that is evil.

———◦❦◦———

I F you cherish and honour your own parents, then do you give your children the most forcible teaching for their duty, *example.* And your duty to your children requires your example to be good in all things. How can you expect counsel to virtue to have any effect, if you constantly contradict it by a bad example? Do not forget, that early impressions are deep and lasting, and from their infancy let them see you keep an upright, noble walk in life, then may you hope to see them follow in your footsteps.

———◦❦◦———

J USTICE, as a sentiment, is inborn, and no one distin-guishes its niceties more quickly than a child. Therefore in your rewards and punishments examine carefully every part of their conduct, and judge calmly, not hastily, and be sure you are just. An unmerited reward will make a child question your judgement as much as an unmerited punishment.

———◦❦◦———

G UARD your temper. Never reprove a child in the heat of passion.

———◦❦◦———

I F your sons see that you regard the rules of politeness in your home, you will find that they treat their mother and sisters with respect and courtesy, and observe, even in play, the rules of etiquette your example teaches; but if you are a domestic tyrant, all your elder and stronger children will strive to act like 'father', by ill-treating or neglecting the younger and weaker ones.

M AKE them, from the moment they begin to talk, use pure and grammatical language, avoid slang phrases, and, above all, profanity. You will find this rule, enforced during childhood, will have more effect than a library full of books or the most unwearied instruction can accomplish, after bad habits in conversation have once been formed.

M AKE them, from early childhood, observe the rules of politeness towards each other. Let your sons treat your daughters as, when men, you would have them treat other females, and let your daughters, by gentleness and love, repay these attentions. You may feel sure that the brothers and sisters, who are polite one to another, will not err in etiquette when abroad.

I N the home circle may very properly be included the humble portion, whose onerous duties are too often repaid by harshness and rudeness; I mean the servants. A true gentleman, while he never allows familiarity from his servants, will always remember that they are human beings, who feel kindness or rudeness as keenly as the more favoured ones up stairs. Chesterfield says: 'There is a certain politeness *due* to your inferiors, and whoever is without it, is without good nature. We do not need to compliment our servants, nor to talk of their doing us the honour, etc., but we ought to treat them with benevolence and mildness.'

'WE are all of the same species, and no distinction whatever is between us, except that which arises from fortune. For example, your footman and cook would be your equals were they as rich as you. Being poor they are obliged to serve you. Therefore, you must not add to their misfortunes by insulting or ill-treating them. If your situation is preferable to theirs, be thankful, without either despising them or being vain of your better fortune. You must, therefore, treat all your inferiors with affability and good manners, and not speak to them in a surly tone, nor with harsh expressions, as if they were of a different species. A good heart never reminds people of their inferiority, but endeavours to alleviate their misfortunes, and make them forget them.'

'EXAMPLE,' says Mrs Parkes, 'is of the greatest importance to our servants, particularly those who are young, whose habits are frequently formed by the first service they enter. With the mild and good, they become softened and improved, but with the dissipated and violent, are too often disorderly and vicious. It is, therefore, not among the least of the duties incumbent on the head of the family, to place in their view such examples as are worthy their imitation. But these examples, otherwise praiseworthy, should neither be rendered disagreeable, nor have their force diminished by any accompaniment of ill humour. Rather by the happiness and comfort resulting from our conduct towards our domestics, should they be made sensible of the beauty of virtue. What we admire, we often strive to imitate, and thus they may be led on to imitate good principles, and to form regular and virtuous habits.'

CHAPTER XIII

True Courtesy

P OLITENESS is the art of pleasing. It is to the deportment what the finer touches of the pencil are to the picture, or what harmony is to music. In the formation of character, it is indispensably requisite. 'We are all,' says Locke, 'a kind of chameleon, that take a tincture from the objects which surround us.' True courtesy, indeed, chiefly consists in accommodating ourselves to the feelings of others, without descending from our own dignity, or denuding ourselves of our own principles. By constant intercourse with society, we acquire what is called politeness almost intuitively, as the shells of the sea are rendered smooth by the unceasing friction of the waves; though there appears to be a natural grace about the well bred, which many feel it difficult to attain.

R ELIGION itself teaches us to honour all men, and to do unto others as we would others do unto us. This includes the whole principle of courtesy, which in this we may remark, assimilates to the principle of justice. It comprises, indeed, all the moral virtues in one, consisting not merely in external show, but having its principle in the heart. The politeness which superficial writers are fond of describing, has been defined as 'the appearance of all the virtues, without possessing one of them'; but by this is meant the mere outward parade, or that kind of artificial adornment of demeanour, which owes its existence to an over-refinement of civility. Anything forced or formal is contrary to the very character of courtesy, which does not consist in a becoming deportment alone, but is prompted and guided by a superior mind, impelling the really polite person to bear with the failings of some, to overlook the weakness of others, and to endure patiently the caprices of all. Indeed, one of the essential characteristics of courtesy is good nature, and an inclination always to look at the bright side of things.

T HE principal rules of politeness are, to subdue the temper, to submit to the weakness of our fellow men, and to render to all their due, freely and courteously. These, with the judgement to recommend ourselves to those whom we meet in society, and the discrimination to know when and to whom to yield, as well as the discretion to treat all with the deference due to their reputation, station, or merit, comprise, in general, the character of a polite man, over which the admission of even one blot or shade will throw a blemish not easily removed.

S INCERITY is another essential characteristic of courtesy; for, without it, the social system would have no permanent foundation or hope of continuance. It is the want of this which makes society, what it is said to be, artificial.

G OOD breeding, in a great measure, consists in being easy, but not indifferent; good humoured, but not familiar; passive, but not unconcerned. It includes, also, a sensibility nice, yet correct; a tact delicate, yet true. There is a beautiful uniformity in the demeanour of a polite man; and it is impossible not to be struck with his affable air. There is a golden mean in the art, which it should be everybody's object to attain, without descending to obsequiousness on the one hand, or to familiarity on the other. In politeness, as in everything else, there is the medium betwixt too much and too little, betwixt constraint and freedom; for civilities carried to extreme are wearisome, and mere ceremony is not politeness, but the reverse.

T HE truly pious people are the truly courteous. 'Religion,' says Leighton, 'is in this mistaken sometimes, in that we think it imprints a roughness and austerity upon the mind and carriage. It doth, indeed, bar all vanity and lightness, and all compliance'; but it softens the manners, tempers the address, and refines the heart.

P RIDE is one of the greatest obstacles to true courtesy that can be mentioned. He who assumes too much on his own merit, shows that he does not understand the simplest principles of politeness. The feeling of pride is, of itself, highly culpable. No man, whether he be a monarch on the throne, or the meanest beggar in his realm, possesses any right to comport himself with a haughty or discourteous air towards his fellow men. The poet truly says: 'What most ennobles human nature, Was ne'er the portion of the proud.'

I T is easy to bestow a kind word, or assume a gracious smile; these will recommend us to every one; while a haughty demeanour, or an austere look, may forfeit forever the favour of those whose good opinion we may be anxious to secure. The really courteous man has a thorough knowledge of human nature, and can make allowances for its weaknesses. He is always consistent with himself. The polite alone know how to make others polite, as the good alone know how to inspire others with a relish for virtue.

H AVING mentioned pride as being opposed to true politeness, I may class affectation with it, in that respect. Affectation is a deviation from, at the same time that it is an imitation of, nature. It is the result of bad taste, and of mistaken notions of one's own qualities. The other vices are limited, and have each a particular object; but affectation pervades the whole conduct, and detracts from the merit of whatever virtues and good dispositions a man may possess. Beauty itself loses its attraction, when disfigured by affectation. Even to copy from the best patterns is improper, because the imitation can never be so good as the original. Counterfeit coin is not so valuable as the real, and when discovered, it cannot pass current. Affectation is a sure sign that there is something to conceal, rather than anything to be proud of, in the character and disposition of the persons practising it.

CHAPTER XIV

Letter Writing

T HERE is no branch of a man's education, no portion of his intercourse with other men, and no quality which will stand him in good stead more frequently than the capability of writing a good letter upon any and every subject. In business, in his intercourse with society, in, I may say, almost every circumstance of his life, he will find his pen called into requisition. Yet, although so important, so almost indispensable an accomplishment, it is one which is but little cultivated, and a letter, perfect in every part, is a great rarity.

I N the composition of a good letter there are many points to be considered, and we take first the simplest and lowest, namely, the spelling.

M ANY spell badly from ignorance, but more from carelessness. The latter, writing rapidly, make, very often, mistakes that would disgrace a schoolboy. If you are in doubt about a word, do not from a feeling of false shame let the spelling stand in its doubtful position hoping that, if wrong, it will pass unnoticed, but get a dictionary, and see what is the correct orthography. Besides the actual misplacing of letters in a word there is another fault of careless, rapid writing, frequently seen. This is to write two words in one, running them together. I have more than once seen *with him* written *withim*, and *for her* stand thus, *forer*. Strange, too, as it may seem, it is more frequently the short, common words that are misspelled than long ones. They flow from the pen mechanically, while over an unaccustomed word the writer unconsciously stops to consider the orthography.

C HESTERFIELD, in his advice to his son, says: 'I come now to another part of your letter, which is the orthography, if I may call bad spelling *orthography*. You spell induce, *enduce*; and grandeur, you spell *grandure*; two faults of which few of my housemaids would have been guilty. I must tell you that orthography, in the true sense of the word, is so absolutely necessary for a man of letters, or a gentleman, that one false spelling may fix ridicule upon him for the rest of his life; and I know a man of quality, who never recovered the ridicule of having spelled *wholesome* without the *w*.'

'R EADING with care will secure everybody from false spelling; for books are always well spelled, according to the orthography of the times. Some words are indeed doubtful, being spelled differently by different authors of equal authority; but those are few; and in those cases every man has his option, because he may plead his authority either way; but where there is but one right way, as in the

two words above mentioned, it is unpardonable and ridiculous for a gentleman to miss it; even a woman of tolerable
education would despise and laugh at a lover, who sent her an
ill-spelled *billet-doux*. I fear, and suspect, that you have taken
it into your head, in most cases, that the matter is all, and
the manner little or nothing. If you have, undeceive yourself,
and be convinced that, in everything, the manner is full as
important as the matter. If you speak the sense of an angel
in bad words, and with a disagreeable utterance, nobody
will hear you twice, who can help it. If you write epistles as
well as Cicero, but in a very bad hand, and very ill-spelled,
whoever receives, will laugh at them.'

A FTER orthography, you should make it a point to write
a good hand; clear, legible, and at the same time easy,
graceful, and rapid. This is not so difficult as some persons
imagine, but, like other accomplishments, it requires practice
to make it perfect. You must write every word so clearly that
it *cannot* be mistaken by the reader, and it is quite an important
requisite to leave sufficient space between the words to render
each one separate and distinct. If your writing is crowded, it
will be difficult to read, even though each letter is perfectly
well formed. An English author, in a letter of advice, says: –

> 'I have often told you that every man who has the use
> of his eyes and his hand can write whatever hand he
> pleases. I do not desire that you should write the stiff,
> laboured characters of a writing master; a man of
> business must write quick and well, and that depends
> simply upon use. I would, therefore, advise you to get
> some very good writing master, and apply to it for

a month only, which will be sufficient; for, upon my word, the writing of a genteel, plain hand of business is of much more importance than you think. You say, it may be, that when you write so very ill, it is because you are in a hurry; to which, I answer, Why are you ever in a hurry? A man of sense may be in haste, but can never be in a hurry, because he knows, that whatever he does in a hurry, he must necessarily do very ill. He may be in haste to dispatch an affair, but he will take care not to let that haste hinder his doing it well. Little minds are in a hurry, when the object proves (as it commonly does) too big for them; they run, they puzzle, confound, and perplex themselves; they want to do everything at once, and never do it at all. But a man of sense takes the time necessary for doing the thing he is about, well; and his haste to dispatch a business, only appears by the continuity of his application to it; he pursues it with a cool steadiness, and finishes it before he begins any other.'

'T HE few seconds that are saved in the course of the day by writing ill instead of well, do not amount to an object of time by any means equivalent to the disgrace or ridicule of a badly written scrawl.'

B Y making a good, clear hand habitual to you, the caution given above, with regard to hurry, will be entirely useless, for you will find that even the most rapid penmanship will not interfere with the beauty of your handwriting, and the most absorbing interest in the subject of your epistle can be indulged; whereas, if you write well only when you are giving your entire attention to guiding your pen, then, haste in writing or interest in your subject will spoil the beauty of your sheet.

———◦⊙◦———

B E very careful that the wording of your letters is in strict accordance with the rules of grammar. Nothing stamps the difference between a well-educated man and an ignorant one more decidedly than the purely grammatical language of the one compared with the laboured sentences, misplaced verbs, nouns, adjectives, and adverbs of the other. Chesterfield caricatures this fault in the following letter, written as a warning to his son, to guard him against its glaring faults:

———◦⊙◦———

'M Y LORD: I *had*, last night, the honour of your Lordship's letter of the 24th; and will *set about doing* the orders contained *therein*; and *if so be* that I can get that affair done by the next post, I will not fail *for to* give your Lordship an account of it, by *next post*. I have told the French Minister, *as how that if* that affair be not soon concluded, your Lordship would think it *all long of him*; and that he must have neglected *for to* have wrote to his court about it. I must beg leave to put your Lordship in mind, *as how*, that I am now full three quarters in arrear; and if *so be* that I do not very soon receive at least one half year, I shall *cut a very bad figure, for this here* place is very dear. I shall be *vastly beholden* to your Lordship for *that there* mark of your favour; and so I *rest* or *remain*, Your, etc.'

THIS is, I admit, a broad burlesque of a letter written by a man holding any important government office, but in the more private correspondence of a man's life letters quite as absurd and ungrammatical are written every day.

PUNCTUATION is another very important point in a letter, because it not only is a mark of elegance and education to properly punctuate a letter, but the omission of this point will inevitably confuse your correspondent, for if you write to your friend: 'I met last evening Mr James the artist his son a lawyer Mr Gay a friend of my mother's Mr Clarke and Mr Paul' he will not know whether Mr Gay is a lawyer or your mother's friend, or whether it is Mr James or his son who is an artist; whereas, by the proper placing of a few punctuation marks you make the sentence clear and intelligible, thus: 'I met, last evening, Mr James, the artist; his son, a lawyer; Mr Gay, a friend of my mother's; Mr Clarke and Mr Paul.'

WITHOUT proper regard being paid to punctuation, the very essence of good composition is lost; it is of the utmost importance, as clearness, strength, and accuracy depend upon it, in as great a measure as the power of an army depends upon the skill displayed in marshalling and arranging the troops. The separation of one portion of a composition from another; the proper classification and division of the subjects; the precise meaning of every word and sentence; the relation each part bears to previous or following parts; the connection of one portion and separation of others – all depend upon punctuation.

———◦◦◦◦———

WE now come to the use of capital letters, a subject next, in importance to punctuation, and one too often neglected, even by writers otherwise careful.

———◦◦◦◦———

THE first word of every piece of writing, whether it be a book, a poem, a story, a letter, a bill, a note, or only a line of directions, must begin with a capital letter.

———◦◦◦◦———

QUOTATIONS, even though they are not immediately preceded by a period, must invariably begin with a capital letter.

———◦◦◦◦———

EVERY new sentence, following a period, exclamation mark, or interrogation point, must begin with a capital letter.

———◦◦◦◦———

EVERY proper name, whether it be of a person, a place, or an object, must begin with a capital letter. The pronoun I and exclamation O must be always written in capital letters.

C APITALS must never, except in the case of proper names or the two letters mentioned in the last paragraph, be written in the middle of a sentence.

A CAPITAL letter must never be used in the middle of a word, among the small letters; nor must it be used at the end of a word.

N OTHING adds more to the beauty of a letter, or any written composition, than handsomely written capital letters, used in their proper places.

H AVING specified the most important points in a correct letter, we next come to that which, more than anything else, shows the mind of the writer; that which proves his good or bad education; that which gives him rank as an elegant or inelegant writer – style.

I T is style which adorns or disfigures a subject; which makes the humblest matter appear choice and elegant, or which reduces the most exalted ideas to a level with common, or vulgar ones.

Lord Chesterfield says, 'It is of the greatest importance to write letters well; as this is a talent which
unavoidably occurs every day of one's life, as well in business
as in pleasure; and inaccuracies in orthography or in style
are never pardoned. Much depends upon the manner in
which they are written; which ought to be easy and natural,
not strained and florid. For instance, when you are about
to send a *billet-doux*, or love letter to a fair friend, you must
only think of what you would say to her if you were both
together, and then write it; that renders the style easy and
natural; though some people imagine the wording of a letter
to be a great undertaking, and think they must write abun-
dantly better than they talk, which is not at all necessary.
Style is the dress of thoughts, and let them be ever so just, if
your style is homely, coarse, and vulgar, they will appear to
as much disadvantage and be as ill received as your person,
though ever so well proportioned, would, if dressed in rags,
dirt, and tatters. It is not every understanding that can judge
of matter; but everyone can and does judge, more or less,
of style; and were I either to speak or write to the public, I
should prefer moderate matter, adorned with all the beauties
and elegancies of style, to the strongest matter in the world,
ill worded and ill delivered.'

Write legibly, correctly, and without erasures upon
a whole sheet of paper, never upon half a sheet.
Choose paper which is thick, white, and perfectly plain. The
initials stamped at the top of a sheet are the only ornament
allowed a gentleman.

I T is an unpardonable fault to write upon a sheet which has anything written or drawn upon it, or is soiled; and quite as bad to answer a note upon half the sheet it is written upon, or write on the other side of a sheet which has been used before.

———⚬⊚⚬———

W RITE your own ideas in your own words, neither borrowing or copying from another. If you are detected in a plagiarism, you will never recover your reputation for originality, and you may find yourself in the position of the hero of the following anecdote:

———⚬⊚⚬———

M R O., a man of but little cultivation, fell in love with Miss N., whose fine intellect was duly improved by a thorough course of study and reading, while her wit, vivacity, and beauty made Mr O. one only amongst many suitors. Fascinated by her beauty and gracious manner he determined to settle his fate, and ask her to go forward in the alphabet and choose the next letter to put to her surname. But how? Five times he tried to speak, and five times the gay beauty so led the discourse that he left at the end of each interview, no wiser than when he came. At length he resolved to write. It was the first time he had held the pen for any but a business letter. After commencing twice with 'Dear sir,' once with, 'I write to inform you that I am well and hope this letter will find you the same,' and once with, 'Your last duly received,' he threw the pen aside in disgust and despair. A love letter was beyond his feeble capacities. Suddenly a brilliant idea struck him. He had lately seen, in turning the leaves of a popular novel, a letter, perhaps a love letter. He procured the book, found the

letter. It was full of fire and passion, words of love, protestations of never failing constancy, and contained an offer of
marriage. With a hand that trembled with ecstasy, O. copied
and signed the letter, sealed, directed, and sent it. The next
day came the answer – simply:

My Friend,

Turn to the next page and you will find the reply.

A.N.

He did so, and found a polite refusal of his suit.

———◦◦◦◦———

THE secret of letter-writing consists in writing as you
would speak. Thus, if you speak well, you will write
well; if you speak ill, you will also write ill.

———◦◦◦◦———

ENDEAVOUR always to write as correctly and properly as
possible. If you have reason to doubt your own spelling,
carefully read and correct every letter before you fold it. An ill-
formed letter is, however, better let alone. You will not improve
it by trying to reform it, and the effort will be plainly visible.

———◦◦◦◦———

LET your style be simple, concise, and clear, entirely void
of pretension, without any phrases written merely for

effect, without useless flowery language, respectful towards superiors, women, and older persons, and it will be well.

———⚬⊙⊙⚬———

A BBREVIATIONS are only permitted in business letters, and in friendly correspondence must never be used.

———⚬⊙⊙⚬———

F IGURES are never to be used excepting when putting a date or a sum of money. In a business letter the money is generally specified both in figures and words, thus: $500 Five hundred dollars.

———⚬⊙⊙⚬———

Y OU may put the name, date, and address of a letter either at the top of the page or at the end. I give a specimen of each style to show my meaning.

Philadelphia
June 25th, 1855.
Mr James Smith,

Dear Sir,
The goods ordered in your letter of the 19th inst. were sent this morning by Adam's Express. We shall be always happy to hear from you, and will promptly fill any further orders.

Yours, truly,
Jones, Brown, & Co.

or,

Dear Sir,
Your favour of the 5th inst. received to day. Will execute your
commissions with pleasure.

Yours, truly,
J. Jones.

Mr James Smith.
Phila., June 25th, 1854.

If you send your own address put it under your own signature, thus:

J. Jones,
17 W— st.,
New-York.

———⚬◦⚬———

THE etiquette of letter-writing, should, as much as possible, be influenced by principles of truth. The superscription and the subscription should alike be in accordance with the tone of the communication, and the domestic or social relation of those between whom it passes. Communications upon professional or business matters, where no acquaintance exists to modify the circumstances, should be written thus: – 'Mr Gillot will feel obliged by Mr Slack's sending by the bearer,' etc. It is an absurdity for a man who writes a challenge, or an offensive letter, to another, to subscribe himself, 'Your obedient Servant'. I dislike this form of subscription, also, when employed by persons of equal rank. It is perfectly becoming when addressed by a servant to an employer. But in other cases, 'Yours truly', 'Yours very truly', 'Your Friend', 'Your sincere Friend', 'Your Well-wisher', 'Your grateful Friend', 'Your affectionate Friend', etc., etc., appears to be much more truthful, and to be more in keeping with the legitimate expression of good feeling. It is impossible to lay down a set of rules that shall govern all cases. But as a principle, it may be urged, that no person should address another as, 'Dear Sir', or, 'Dear Madam', without feelings and relations that justify the use of the adjective. These compliments are mockeries. No one who entertains a desire to write another as 'dear', need feel afraid of giving offence by familiarity; for all mankind prize the esteem even of their humblest fellows too much to be annoyed by it. And in proportion as the integrity of the forms of correspondence increase, so will these expressions of good feeling be more appreciated.

THE next point to be considered is the *subject* of your letter, and without a good subject the epistle will be apt to be dull. I do not mean by this that it is necessary to have any extraordinary event to relate, or startling news to communicate; but in order to write a *good* letter, it is necessary to have a *good* subject, that you may not rival the Frenchman who wrote to his wife – 'I write to you because I have nothing to do: I stop because I have nothing to say.' Letters written without aim or object, simply for the sake of writing, are apt to be stupid, trivial, or foolish.

Y OU may write to a friend to congratulate him upon some happy event to himself, or to condole with him in some misfortune, or to ask his congratulations or condolence for yourself. You may write to enquire for his health, or to extend an invitation, a letter of thanks, felicitations, upon business, or a thousand other subjects, which it is useless for me to enumerate.

L ETTERS OF BUSINESS. The chief object in a letter of business is to communicate or enquire about some one fact, and the epistle should be confined entirely to that fact. All compliments, jests, high-flown language and sentiment, are entirely out of place in a business letter, and brevity should be one of the most important aims. Do not let your desire to be brief, however, make your meaning obscure; better to add a few words, or even lines, to the length of your letter, than to send it in confused, unintelligible language. Chesterfield's advice on business letters is excellent. He says:

'T HE first thing necessary in writing letters of business is, extreme clearness and perspicuity; every paragraph should be so clear and unambiguous that the dullest fellow in the world may not be able to mistake it, nor obliged to read it twice in order to understand it. This necessary clearness implies a correctness, without excluding an elegance of style. Tropes, figures, antithesis, epigrams, etc., would be as misplaced and as impertinent in letters of business as they are sometimes (if judiciously used) proper and pleasing in familiar letters, upon common and trite subjects. In business, an elegant simplicity, the result of care, not of labour, is required. Business must be well, not affectedly dressed; but by no means negligently. Let your first attention be to clearness, and read every paragraph after you have written it, in the critical view of discovering whether it is possible that any one man can mistake the true sense of it; and correct it accordingly.'

L ETTERS OF ENQUIRY should be written in a happy medium, between tedious length and the brevity which would betoken indifference. As the subject is generally limited to questions upon one subject, they will not admit of much verbiage, and if your enquiry relates simply to a matter of business, it is better to confine your words strictly to that business; if, however, you are writing to make enquiry as to the health of a friend, or any other matter in which feeling or affection dictates the epistle, the cold, formal style of a business letter would become heartless, and, in many cases, positively insulting. You must here add some words of compliment, express your friendly interest in the subject, and your hope that a favourable answer may be returned, and if the occasion is a painful one, a few lines of regret or condolence may be added.

I F you are requesting a favour of your correspondent, you should apologise for the trouble you are giving him, and mention the necessity which prompts you to write.

I f you are making enquiries of a friend, your letter will then admit of some words of compliment, and may be written in an easy, familiar style.

---❦---

I f writing to a stranger, your request for information becomes a personal favour, and you should write in a manner to show him that you feel this. Speak of the obligation he will confer, mention the necessity which compels you to trouble him, and follow his answer by a note of thanks.

---❦---

A lways, when sending a letter of enquiry, enclose a stamp for the answer. If you trouble your correspondent to take his time to write you information, valuable only to yourself, you have no right to tax him also for the price of postage.

---❦---

A nswers to letters of Enquiry should be written as soon as possible after such letters are received. If the enquiry is of a personal nature, concerning your health, family affairs, or the denial or corroboration of some report concerning yourself, you should thank your correspondent for the interest he expresses, and such a letter should be answered immediately. If the letter you receive contains questions which you cannot answer instantly, as, for instance, if you are obliged to see a third party, or yourself make enquiry upon the subject proposed, it is best to write a few lines acknowledging the receipt of your friend's letter, expressing your pleasure at being able to serve him, and stating why you cannot immediately give him the desired information, with the promise to write again as soon as such information is yours to send.

———◦◦◦———

LETTERS REQUESTING FAVOURS are trying to write, and must be dictated by the circumstances which make them necessary. Be careful not to be servile in such letters. Take a respectful, but, at the same time, manly tone; and, while you acknowledge the obligation a favourable answer will confer, do not adopt the cringing language of a beggar.

———◦◦◦———

LETTERS CONFERRING FAVOURS should never be written in a style to make the recipient feel a weight of obligation; on the contrary, the style should be such as will endeavour to convince your correspondent that in his acceptance of your favour *he* confers an obligation upon *you*.

———◦◦◦———

LETTERS REFUSING FAVOURS call for your most cour- teous language, for they must give some pain, and this may be very much softened by the manner in which you write. Express your regret at being unable to grant your friend's request, a hope that at some future time it may be in your power to answer another such letter more favourably, and give a good reason for your refusal.

———◦◦◦———

L ETTERS ACKNOWLEDGING FAVOURS, or letters of thanks, should be written in a cordial, frank, and grateful style. While you earnestly thank your correspondent for his kindness, you must never hint at any payment of the obligation. If you have the means of obliging him near you at that instant, make your offer of the favour the subject of another letter, lest he attribute your haste to a desire to rid yourself of an obligation. To hint at a future payment is still more indelicate. When you can show your gratitude by a suitable return, then let your actions, not your words, speak for the accuracy of your memory in retaining the recollection of favours conferred.

L ETTERS OF INTELLIGENCE. The first thing to be regarded in a letter of intelligence is *truth*. They are written on every variety of subjects, under circumstances of the saddest and the most joyful nature. They are written often under the pressure of the most crushing grief, at other times when the hand trembles with ecstasy, and very frequently when a weight of other cares and engagements makes the time of the writer invaluable. Yet, whether the subject communicated concerns yourself or another, remember that every written word is a record for your veracity or falsehood. If exaggeration, or, still worse, malice, guide your pen, in imparting painful subjects, or if the desire to avoid causing grief makes you violate truth to soften trying news, you are signing your name to a written falsehood, and the letter may, at some future time, rise to confront you and prove that your intelligence cannot be trusted. Whatever the character of the news you communicate, let taste and discretion guide you in the manner of imparting it. If it is of so sorrowful a character that you know it must cause pain, you may endeavour to open the subject gradually, and a few lines of sympathy and comfort, if unheeded at the time, may be appreciated when the mourner rereads your letter in calmer moments. Joyful news, though it does not need the same caution, also admits of expressions of sympathy.

NEVER write the gossip around you, unless you are obliged to communicate some event, and then write only what you know to be true, or, if you speak of doubtful matters, state them to be such. Avoid mere scandal and hearsay, and, above all, avoid letting your own malice or bitterness of feeling colour all your statements in their blackest dye. Be, under such circumstances, truthful, just, and charitable.

LETTERS OF RECOMMENDATION should be written only when they are positively necessary, and great caution should be used in giving them. They make you, in a measure, responsible for the conduct of another, and if you give them frequently, on slight grounds, you will certainly have cause to repent your carelessness. They are letters of business, and should be carefully composed; truthful, while they are courteous, and just, while they are kind. If you sacrifice candour to a mistaken kindness, you not only make yourself a party to any mischief that may result, but you are committing a dishonest act towards the person to whom the letter will be delivered.

Anonymous Letters. The man who would write an anonymous letter, either to insult the person addressed, or annoy a third person, is a scoundrel, 'whom 'twere gross flattery to name a coward'. None but a man of the lowest principles, and meanest character, would commit an act to gratify malice or hatred without danger to himself. A gentleman will treat such a communication with the contemptuous silence which it deserves.

Letters of Introduction should be short, as they are generally delivered in person, and ought not to occupy much time in reading, as no one likes to have to wait while a long letter of introduction is read. While you speak of the bearer in the warm language of friendship, do not write praises in such a letter; they are about as much in place as they would be if you spoke them at a personal introduction. Leave letters of introduction unsealed, for it is a gross breach of politeness to prevent the bearer from reading what you have written, by fastening the envelope. The most common form is: –

Dear Sir,

It gives me much pleasure to introduce to you, the bearer of this letter, as my friend Mr. F—, who is to remain a few days in your city on his way to New Orleans. I trust that the acquaintance of two friends, for whom I have so long entertained so warm an esteem, will prove as pleasant as my intercourse with each has always been. Any attention which it may be in your power to pay to Mr J—, whilst he is in your city, will be highly appreciated and gratefully acknowledged

by

Your sincere friend
James C. Ray.

Mr L. G. Edmonds.
June 23d, 18 - .

I F your letter is to introduce any gentleman in his business or professional capacity, mention what that business is; and if your own acquaintance with the bearer is slight, you may also use the name of the persons from whom he brought letters to yourself. Here, you may, with perfect propriety, say a few words in praise of the bearer's skill in his professional labours. If he is an artist, you need not hesitate to give a favourable opinion of whatever of his pictures you have seen, or, if a musician, express the delight his skill has afforded you.

A LETTER REQUESTING AN AUTOGRAPH should always enclose a postage stamp for the reply. In such a letter some words of compliment, expressive of the value of the name for which you ask, is in good taste. You may refer to the deeds or celebrity which have made the name so desirable, and also express your sense of the greatness of the favour, and the obligation the granting of it will confer.

AUTOGRAPH LETTERS should be short; containing merely a few lines, thanking the person addressed for the compliment paid in requesting the signature, and expressive of the pleasure it gives you to comply with the request. If you wish to refuse (though none but a churl would do so), do not fall into the error of an eccentric American whose high position in the army tempted a collector of autographs to request his signature. The general wrote in reply: –

Sir,

I'll be hanged if I send my autograph to anybody.

Yours,

and signed his name in full in the strong, bold letters which always characterised his hand writing.

INVITATIONS TO LADIES should be written in the third person, unless you are very intimate with them, or can claim relationship. All letters addressed to a lady should be written in a respectful style, and when they are short and to a comparative stranger, the third person is the most elegant one to use. Remember, in directing letters to young ladies, the eldest one in a family is addressed by the surname alone, while the others have also the proper name; thus, if you wrote to the daughters of Mr Smith, the eldest one is Miss

Smith, the others, Miss Annie Smith and Miss Jane Smith. Invitations should be sent by your own servant, or clerk. Nothing is more vulgar than sending invitations through the despatch, and you run the risk of their being delayed. The first time that you invite a lady to accompany you to ride, walk, or visit any place of public amusement, you should also invite her mother, sister, or any other lady in the same family, unless you have a mother or sister with whom the lady invited is acquainted, when you should say in your note that your mother or sister will accompany you.

———⁜———

L ETTERS OF COMPLIMENT being confined to one subject should be short and simple. If they are of thanks for enquiry made, they should merely echo the letter they answer, with the acknowledgement of your correspondent's courtesy.

———⁜———

L ETTERS OF CONGRATULATION. Letters of congratu-lation are the most agreeable of all letters to write; your subject is before you, and you have the pleasure of sympa-thising in the happiness of a friend. They should be written in a frank, genial style, with warm expressions of pleasure at your friend's joy, and admit of any happy quotations or jest.

———⁜———

W HEN congratulating your friend on an occasion of happiness to himself, be very careful that your letter has no word of envy at his good fortune, no fears for its short duration, no prophecy of a change for the worse; let all be bright, cheerful, and hopeful. There are few men whose life calls for letters of congratulation upon many occasions, let them have bright, unclouded ones when they can claim them. If you have other friends whose sorrow makes a contrast with the joy of the person to whom you are writing, nay, even if you yourself are in affliction, do not mention it in such a letter.

⸻

L ETTERS OF CONDOLENCE are trying both to the writer and to the reader. If your sympathy is sincere, and you feel the grief of your friend as if it were your own, you will find it difficult to express in written words the sorrow that you are anxious to comfort.

⸻

E VEN the warmest, most sincere expressions, sound cold and commonplace to the mourner, and one grasp of the hand, one glance of the eye, will do more to express sympathy than whole sheets of written words. It is best not to try to say *all* that you feel. You will fail in the attempt and may weary your friend. Let your letter, then, be short, (not heartlessly so) but let its words, though few, be warm and sincere. Any light, cheerful jesting will be insulting in a letter of condolence. If you wish to comfort by bringing forward blessings or hopes for the future, do not do it with gay, or jesting expressions, but in a gentle, kind manner, drawing your words of comfort, not from trivial, passing events, but from the highest and purest sources.

⸻

IF the subject for condolence be loss of fortune or any similar event, your letter will admit of the cheering words of everyday life, and kindly hopes that the wheel of fortune may take a more favourable turn; but, if death causes your friend's affliction, there is but little to be said in the first hours of grief. Your letter of sympathy and comfort may be read after the first crushing grief is over, and appreciated then, but words of comfort are but little heeded when the first agony of a life-long separation is felt in all the force of its first hours.

LETTERS ACKNOWLEDGING PRESENTS should also be quite short, written in the third person, and merely containing a few lines of thanks, with a word or two of admiration for the beauty, value, or usefulness of the gift.

LETTERS OF ADVICE are generally very unpalatable for the reader, and had better not be written unless solicited, and not then unless your counsel will really benefit your correspondent. When written, let them be courteous, but, at the same time, perfectly frank. If you can avert an evil by writing a letter of advice, even when unsolicited, it is a friendly office to write, but it is usually a thankless one.

TO write after an act has been performed, and state what your advice would have been, had your opinion been asked, is extremely foolish, and if you disapprove of the course that has been taken, your best plan is, certainly, to say nothing about it.

I N writing your letter of advice, give your judgement as an opinion, not a law, and say candidly that you will not feel hurt if contrary advice offered by any other, more competent to judge in the case, is taken. While your candour may force you to give the most unpalatable counsel, let your courtesy so express it, that it cannot give offence.

L ETTERS OF EXCUSE are sometimes necessary, and they should be written promptly, as a late apology for an offence is worse than no apology at all. They should be written in a frank, manly style, containing an explanation of the offence, and the facts which led to it, the assurance of the absence of malice or desire to offend, sorrow for the circumstances, and a hope that your apology will be accepted. Never wait until circumstances force an apology from you before writing a letter of excuse. A frank, prompt acknowledgement of an offence, and a candidly expressed desire to atone for it, or for indulgence towards it, cannot fail to conciliate any reasonable person.

CHAPTER XV

Wedding Etiquette

FROM an English work, *The Habits of Good Society*, I quote some directions for the guidance of the happy man who proposes to enter the state of matrimony. I have altered a few words to suit the difference of country, but when weddings are performed in church, the rules given here are excellent. They will apply equally well to the evening ceremony.

'AT a time when our feelings are or ought to be most susceptible, when the happiness or misery of a condition in which there is no medium begins, we are surrounded with forms and etiquettes which rise before the unwary like spectres, and which even the most rigid ceremonialists regard with a sort of dread.'

'WERE it not, however, for these forms, and for this necessity of being *en règle*, there might, on the solemnisation of marriage, be confusion, forgetfulness, and, even – speak it not aloud – irritation among the parties most intimately concerned. Excitement might ruin all. Without a definite programme, the old maids of the family would be thrusting in advice. The aged chronicler of past events, or grandmother by the fireside, would have it all her way; the venerable bachelor in tights, with his blue coat and metal buttons, might throw everything into confusion by his suggestions. It is well that we are independent of all these interfering advisers; that there is no necessity to appeal to them. Precedent has arranged it all; we have only to put in or understand what that stern authority has laid down; how it has been varied by modern changes; and we must just shape our course boldly. "Boldly?" But there is much to be done before we come to that. First, there is the offer to be made. Well may a man who contemplates such a step say to himself, with Dryden: "These are the realms of everlasting fate" for, in truth, on marriage one's well-being not only here but even hereafter mainly depends. But it is not on this bearing of the subject that we wish to enter, contenting ourselves with a quotation from the *Spectator.* "It requires more virtues to make a good husband or wife, than what go to the finishing any the most shining character whatsoever."'

———•◦◦◦•———

'IN France, an engagement is an affair of negotiation and business; and the system, in this respect, greatly resembles the practice in England, on similar occasions, a hundred and fifty or two hundred years ago, or even later. France is the most unchanging country in the world in her habits and domestic institutions, and foremost among these is her "*Marriage de convenance*", or "*Marriage de raison*".'

———•◦◦◦•———

'I T is thus brought about. So soon as a young girl quits the school or convent where she has been educated, her friends cast about for a suitable *parti*. Most parents in France take care, so soon as a daughter is born, to put aside a sum of money for her "*dot*", as they well know that, whatever may be her attractions, *that* is indispensable in order to be married. They are ever on the lookout for a youth with, at least, an equal fortune, or more; or, if they are rich, for title, which is deemed tantamount to fortune; even the power of writing those two little letters *De* before your name has some value in the marriage contract. Having satisfied themselves, they thus address the young lady: "It is now time for you to be married; I know of an eligible match; you can see the gentleman, either at such a ball, or [if he is serious] at church. I do not ask you to take him if his appearance is positively disagreeable to you; if so, we will look out for someone else."'

'A s a matter of custom, the young lady answers that the will of her parents is hers; she consents to take a survey of him to whom her destiny is to be entrusted; and let us presume that he is accepted, though it does not follow, and sometimes it takes several months to look out, as it does for other matters, a house, or a place, or a pair of horses. However, she consents; a formal introduction takes place; the *promis* calls in full dress to see his future wife; they are only just to speak to each other, and those few unmeaning words are spoken in the presence of the bride-elect's mother; for the French think it most indiscreet to allow the affections of a girl to be interested before marriage, lest during the arrangements for the contract all should be broken off. If she has no dislike, it is enough; never for an instant are the engaged couple left alone, and in very few cases do they go up to the altar with more than a few weeks' acquaintance, and usually with less. The whole matter is then arranged by notaries, who squabble over the marriage-contract, and get all they can for their clients.'

⁕⊙⊙⁕

'THE contract is usually signed in France on the day before the marriage, when all is considered safe; the religious portion of their bond takes place in the church, and then the two young creatures are left together to understand each other if they can, and to love each other if they will; if not they must content themselves with what is termed, *un ménage de Paris*.'

⁕⊙⊙⁕

'IN England, formerly, much the same system prevailed. A boy of fourteen, before going on his travels, was contracted to a girl of eleven, selected as his future wife by parents or guardians; he came back after the *grande tour* to fulfil the engagement. But by law it was imperative that forty days should at least pass between the contract and the marriage; during which dreary interval the couple, leashed together like two young greyhounds, would have time to think of the future. In France, the perilous period of reflection is not allowed. "I really am so glad we are to take a journey," said a young French lady to her friends; "I shall thus get to know something about my husband; he is quite a stranger to me." Some striking instances of the *Marriage de convenance* being infringed on, have lately occurred in France. The late Monsieur de Tocqueville married for love, after a five years' engagement. Guizot, probably influenced by his acquaintance with England, gave his daughters liberty to choose for themselves, and they married for love – "a very indelicate proceeding", remarked a French comtesse of the old *régime*, when speaking of this arrangement.'

'NOTHING can be more opposed to all this than the American system. They are so tenacious of the freedom of choice, that even persuasion is thought criminal. In France negotiations are often commenced on the lady's side; in America, never. Even too encouraging a manner, even the ordinary attentions of civility, are, occasionally, a matter of reproach. We are jealous of the delicacy of that sacred bond; which we presume to hope is to spring out of mutual affection. A gentleman who, from whatever motives, has made up his mind to marry, may set about it in two ways. He may propose by letter or in words. The customs of society imply the necessity of a sufficient knowledge of the lady to be addressed. This, even in this country, is a difficult point to be attained; and, after all, cannot be calculated by time, since, in large cities, you may know people a year, and yet be comparative strangers; and, meeting them in the country, may become intimate in a week.'

'HAVING made up his mind, the gentleman offers – wisely, if he can, in speech. Letters are seldom expressive of what really passes in the mind of man; or, if expressive, seem foolish, since deep feelings are liable to exaggeration. Every written word may be the theme of cavil. Study, care, which avail in every other species of composition, are death to the lover's effusion. A few sentences, spoken in earnest, and broken by emotion, are more eloquent than pages of sentiment, both to parent and daughter. Let him, however, speak and be accepted. He is, in that case, instantly taken into the intimacy of his adopted relatives. Such is the notion of American honour, that the engaged couple are henceforth allowed to be frequently alone together, in walking and at home. If there be no known obstacle to the engagement, the gentleman and lady are mutually introduced to the respective relatives of each. It is for the gentleman's family to call first; for him to make the first present; and this should be done as soon as possible after the offer has been accepted. It is a sort of seal put upon the affair. The absence of presents is thought to imply want of earnestness in the matter. This present generally consists of some personal ornament, say, a ring, and should be handsome, but not so handsome as that made for the wedding day. During the period that elapses before the marriage, the betrothed man should conduct himself with peculiar deference to the lady's family and friends, even if beneath his own station. It is often said: "I marry such a lady, but I do not mean to marry her whole family." This disrespectful pleasantry has something in it so cold, so selfish, that even if the lady's family be disagreeable, there is a total absence of delicate feeling to her in thus speaking of those nearest to her. To her parents especially, the conduct of the betrothed man should be respectful; to her sisters kind without familiarity; to her brothers, every evidence of good-will should be testified. In making every provision for the future, in regard to settlements, allowance for dress, etc., the *extent* of liberality convenient should be the spirit of all arrangements. Perfect candour as to his own affairs, respectful consideration for those of the family he is about to enter, mark a true gentleman.'

'I N France, however gay and even blameable a man may have been before his betrothal, he conducts himself with the utmost propriety after that event. A sense of what is due to a lady should repress all habits unpleasant to her; smoking, if disagreeable; frequenting places of amusement without her; or paying attention to other women. In this respect, indeed, the sense of honour should lead a man to be as scrupulous when his future wife is absent as when she is present, if not more so.'

'I N equally bad taste is exclusiveness. The devotions of two engaged persons should be reserved for the *tête-à-tête*, and women are generally in fault when it is otherwise. They like to exhibit their conquest; they cannot dispense with attentions; they forget that the demonstration of any peculiar condition of things in society must make someone uncomfortable; the young lady is uncomfortable because she is not equally happy; the young man detests what he calls nonsense; the old think there is a time for all things. All sitting apart, therefore, and peculiar displays, are in bad taste; I am inclined to think that they often accompany insincerity, and that the truest affections are those which are reserved for the genuine and heartfelt intimacy of private interviews. At the same time, the airs of indifference and avoidance should be equally guarded against; since, however strong and mutual attachment may be, such a line of conduct is apt needlessly to mislead others, and so produce mischief. True feeling, and a ladylike consideration for others, a point in which the present generation essentially fails, are the best guides for steering between the extremes of demonstration on the one hand, and of frigidity on the other.'

'DURING the arrangement of pecuniary matters, a young lady should endeavour to understand what is going on, receiving it in a right spirit. If she has fortune, she should, in all points left to her, be generous and confiding, at the same time prudent. Many a man, she should remember, may abound in excellent qualities, and yet be improvident. He may mean to do well, yet have a passion for building; he may be the very soul of good nature, yet fond of the gaming-table; he may have no wrong propensities of that sort, and yet have a confused notion of accounts, and be one of those men who muddle away a great deal of money, no one knows how; or he may be a too strict economist, a man who takes too good care of the pence, till he tires your very life out about an extra dollar; or he may be facile or weakly good-natured, and have a friend who preys on him, and for whom he is disposed to become security. Finally, the beloved Charles, Henry, or Reginald may have none of these propensities, but may chance to be an honest merchant, or a tradesman, with all his floating capital in business, and a consequent risk of being one day rich, the next a pauper.'

'UPON every account, therefore, it is desirable for a young lady to have a settlement on her; and she should not, from a weak spirit of romance, oppose her friends who advise it, since it is for her husband's advantage as well as her own. By making a settlement there is always a fund which cannot be touched – a something, however small, as a provision for a wife and children; and whether she have fortune or not, this ought to be made. An allowance for dress should also be arranged; and this should be administered in such a way that a wife should not have to ask for it at inconvenient hours, and thus irritate her husband.'

'EVERY preliminary being settled, there remains nothing except to fix the marriage-day, a point always left to the lady to advance; and next to settle how the ceremonial is to be performed is the subject of consideration.'

'IT is to be lamented that, previous to so solemn a ceremony, the thoughts of the lady concerned must necessarily be engaged for some time upon her *trousseau*. The *trousseau* consists, in this country, of all the habiliments necessary for a lady's use for the first two or three years of her married life; like every other outfit there are always a number of articles introduced into it that are next to useless, and are only calculated for the vain-glory of the ostentatious.'

'THE *trousseau* being completed, and the day fixed, it becomes necessary to select the bridesmaids and the bridegroom's man, and to invite the guests.'

'THE bridesmaids are from two to eight in number. It is ridiculous to have many, as the real intention of the bridesmaid is, that she should act as a witness of the marriage. It is, however, thought a compliment to include the bride's sisters and those of the bridegroom's relations and intimate friends, in case sisters do not exist.'

'WHEN a bride is young the bridesmaids should be young; but it is absurd to see a "single woman of a certain age", or a widow, surrounded by blooming girls, making her look plain and foolish. For them the discreet woman of thirty-five is more suitable as a bridesmaid. Custom decides that the bridesmaids should be spinsters, but there is no legal objection to a married woman being a bridesmaid, should it be necessary, as it might be abroad, or at sea, or where ladies are few in number. Great care should be taken not to give offence in the choice of bridesmaids by a preference, which is always in bad taste on momentous occasions.'

'THE guests at the wedding should be selected with similar attention to what is right and kind, with consideration to those who have a claim on us, not only to what we ourselves prefer.'

'FOR a great wedding breakfast, it is customary to send out printed cards from the parents or guardians from whose house the young lady is to be married.'

'EARLY in the day, before eleven, the bride should be dressed, taking breakfast in her own room. In America they load a bride with lace flounces on a rich silk, and even sometimes with ornaments. In France it is always remembered, with better taste, that when a young lady goes up to the altar, she is "*encore jeune fille*"; her dress, therefore, is exquisitely simple; a dress of tulle over white silk, a long, wide veil of white tulle, going down to the very feet, a wreath of maiden-blush-roses interspersed with orange flowers. This is the usual costume of a French bride of rank, or in the middle classes equally.'

'THE gentleman's dress should differ little from his full morning costume. The days are gone by when gentlemen were married – as a recently deceased friend of mine was – in white satin breeches and waistcoat. In these days men show less joy in their attire at the fond consummation of their hopes, and more in their faces. A dark-blue frock-coat – black being superstitiously considered ominous – a white waistcoat, and a pair of light trousers, suffice for the "happy man". The necktie also should be light and simple. Polished boots are not amiss, though plain ones are better. The gloves must be as white as the linen. Both are typical – for in these days types are as important as under the Hebrew law-givers – of the purity of mind and heart which are supposed to exist in their wearer. Eheu! after all, he cannot be too well dressed, for the more gay he is the greater the compliment to his bride. Flowers in the button-hole and a smile on the face show the bridegroom to be really a "happy man".'

———◦◦◦◦———

'As soon as the carriages are at the door, those bridesmaids who happen to be in the house and the other members of the family set off first. The bride goes last, with her father and mother, or with her mother alone, and the brother or relative who is to represent her father in case of death or absence. The bridegroom, his friend, or bridegroom's man, and the bridesmaids ought to be waiting in the church. The father of the bride gives her his arm, and leads her to the altar. Here her bridesmaids stand near her, as arranged by the clerk, and the bridegroom takes his appointed place.'

———◦◦◦◦———

'It is a good thing for the bridegroom's man to distribute the different fees to the clergyman or clergymen, the clerk, and pew-opener, before the arrival of the bride, as it prevents confusion afterwards.'

———◦◦◦◦———

'The bride stands to the left of the bridegroom, and takes the glove off her right hand, whilst he takes his glove off his right hand. The bride gives her glove to the bridesmaid to hold, and sometimes to keep, as a good omen.'

———◦◦◦◦———

'The service then begins. During the recital, it is certainly a matter of feeling how the parties concerned should behave; but if tears can be restrained, and a quiet modesty in the lady displayed, and her emotions subdued, it adds much

to the gratification of others, and saves a few pangs to the
parents from whom she is to part.'

———◦◦◦———

'IT should be remembered that this is but the closing
scene of a drama of some duration – first the offer, then
the consent and engagement. In most cases the marriage
has been preceded by acts which have stamped the whole
with certainty, although we do not adopt the contract system
of our forefathers, and although no event in this life can be
certain.'

———◦◦◦———

'I HAVE omitted the mention of the bouquet, because it
seems to me always an awkward addition to the bride,
and that it should be presented afterwards on her return to
the breakfast. Gardenias, if in season, white azalia, or even
camellias, with very little orange flowers, form the bridal
bouquet. The bridesmaids are dressed, on this occasion, so
as to complete the picture with effect. When there are six
or eight, it is usual for three of them to dress in one colour,
and three in another. At some of the most fashionable
weddings in London, the bridesmaids wear veils – these are
usually of net or tulle; white tarlatan dresses, over muslin
or beautifully-worked dresses, are much worn, with colours
introduced – pink or blue, and scarves of those colours; and
white bonnets, if bonnets are worn, trimmed with flowers
to correspond. These should be simple, but the flowers as
natural as possible, and of the finest quality. The bouquets of
the bridesmaids should be of mixed flowers. These they may
have at church, but the present custom is for the gentlemen

of the house to present them on their return home, previous
to the wedding breakfast.'

———❦———

'THE register is then signed. The bride quits the church
first with the bridegroom, and gets into his carriage,
and the father and mother, bridesmaids, and bridegroom's
man, follow in order in their own.'

———❦———

'THE breakfast is arranged on one or more tables, and
is generally provided by a confectioner when expense
is not an object.'

———❦———

'PRESENTS are usual, first from the bridegroom to the
bridesmaids. These generally consist of jewellery, the
device of which should be unique or quaint, the article more
elegant than massive. The female servants of the family,
more especially servants who have lived many years in their
place, also expect presents, such as gowns or shawls; or to
a very valued personal attendant or housekeeper, a watch.
But on such points discretion must suggest, and liberality
measure out the *largesse* of the gift.'

———❦———

'WHEN the ceremony is performed at the house of the
bride, the bridegroom should be ready full half an
hour before the time appointed, and enter the parlour at

the head of his army of bridesmaids and groomsmen, with his fair bride on his arm. In America a groomsman is allowed for each bridesmaid, whilst in England one poor man is all that is allowed for six, sometimes eight bridesmaids. The brothers or very intimate friends of the bride and groom are usually selected for groomsmen.'

CHAPTER XVI

Etiquette for Places of Amusement

WHEN you wish to invite a lady to accompany you to the theatre, opera, a concert, or any other public place of amusement, send the invitation the day previous to the one selected for taking her, and write it in the third person. If it is the first time you have invited her, include her mother, sister, or some other lady in the invitation.

IF she accepts your invitation, let it be your next care to secure good seats, for it is but a poor compliment to invite a lady to go to the opera, and put her in an uncomfortable seat, where she can neither hear, see, nor be seen.

ALTHOUGH, when alone, you will act a courteous part in giving your seat to a strange lady, who is standing, in a crowded concert room, you should not do so when you are with a lady. By giving up your place beside her, you may place a lady next her, whom she will find an unpleasant companion, and you are yourself separated from her, when the conversation between the acts makes one of the greatest pleasures of an evening spent in this way. In case of accident, too, he deprives her of his protection, and gives her the appearance of having come alone. Your first duty, when you are escorting a lady, is to that lady before all others.

W HEN you are with a lady at a place of amusement, you must not leave your seat until you rise to escort her home. If at the opera, you may invite her to promenade between the acts, but if she declines, do you too remain in your seat.

L ET all your conversation be in a low tone, not whispered, nor with any air of mystery, but in a tone that will not disturb those seated near you.

A NY lover-like airs or attitudes, although you may have the right to assume them, are in excessively bad taste in public.

I F the evening you have appointed be a stormy one, you must call for your companion with a carriage, and this is the more elegant way of taking her even if the weather does not make it absolutely necessary.

W HEN you are entering a concert room, or the box of a theatre, walk before your companion up the aisle, until you reach the seats you have secured, then turn, offer your hand to her, and place her in the inner seat, taking the outside one yourself; in going out, if the aisle is too narrow to walk two abreast, you again precede your companion until you reach the lobby, where you turn and offer your arm to her.

L OUD talking, laughter, or mistimed applause, are all in very bad taste, for if you do not wish to pay strict attention to the performance, those around you probably do, and you pay but a poor compliment to your companion in thus implying her want of interest in what she came to see.

S ECURE your programme, libretto, or concert bill, before taking your seat, as, if you leave it, in order to obtain them, you may find someone else occupying your place when you return, and when the seats are not secured, he may refuse to rise, thus giving you the alternative of an alter-cation, or leaving your companion without any protector. Or, you may find a lady in your seat, in which case, you have no alternative, but must accept the penalty of your carelessness, by standing all the evening.

I N a crowd, do not push forward, unheeding whom you hurt or inconvenience, but try to protect your companion, as far as possible, and be content to take your turn.

I F your seats are secured, call for your companion in time to be seated some three or four minutes before the performance commences, but if you are visiting a hall where you cannot engage seats, it is best to go early.

I F you are alone and see ladies present with whom you are acquainted, you may, with perfect propriety, go and chat with them between the acts, but when with a lady, never leave her to speak to another lady.

A T an exhibition of pictures or statuary, you may converse, but let it be in a quiet, gentlemanly tone, and without gesture or loud laughter. If you stand long before one picture or statue, see that you are not interfering with others who may wish to see the same work of art. If you are engaged in conversation, and wish to rest, do not take a position that will prevent others from seeing any of the paintings, but sit down, or stand near the centre of the room.

NEVER, unless urgently solicited, attach yourself to any party at a place of amusement, even if some of the members of it are your own relatives or intimate friends.

CHAPTER XVII

Miscellaneous

WHEN you are walking with a lady who has your arm, be careful to *keep step* with her, and do not force her to take long, unladylike steps, or trot beside you with two steps to one of yours, by keeping your usual manly stride.

NEVER allow a lady, with whom you are walking, to carry a bundle, shawl, or bag, unless both your hands are already occupied in her service.

WHEN you attend a wedding or bridal reception, it is the bridegroom whom you are to *congratulate*, offering to the bride your wishes for her future happiness, but not *congratulation*. If you are acquainted with the bridegroom, but not with the bride, speak to him first, and he will introduce you to his bride, but in any other case, you must speak first to the bride, then to the bridegroom, then the bridesmaids, if you have any previous acquaintance with them, then to the parents and family of the bride, and after all this you are at liberty to seek your other friends among the guests. If you are personally a stranger to the newly married couple, but have received a card from being a friend of one of the families or from any other reason, it is the first grooms-man's place to introduce you, and you should give him your card, or mention your name, before he leads you to the bride.

A LWAYS remove a chair or stool that stands in the way of a lady passing, even though she is an entire stranger to you.

Y OU may hand a chair to a strange lady, in a hotel, or upon a boat; you may hand her water, if you see her rise to obtain it, and at a hotel table you may pass her the dishes near you, with perfect propriety.

I N this country where every other man uses tobacco, it may not be amiss to say a few words on smoking.

Dr Prout says, 'Tobacco is confessedly one of the most virulent poisons in nature. Yet such is the fascinating influence of this noxious weed, that mankind resort to it in every form they can devise, to ensure its stupifying and pernicious agency. Tobacco disorders the assimilating functions in general, but particularly, as I believe, the assimilation of the saccharine principle. I have never, indeed, been able to trace the development of oxalic acid to the use of tobacco; but that some analogous, and equally poisonous principle (probably of an acid nature), is generated in certain individuals by its abuse, is evident from their cachectic looks, and from the dark, and often greenish yellow tint of the blood. The severe and peculiar dyspeptic symptoms sometimes produced by inveterate snuff-taking are well known; and I have more than once seen such cases terminate fatally with malignant disease of the stomach and liver. Great smokers, also, especially those who employ short pipes and cigars, are said to be liable to cancerous affections of the lips.'

A<small>N</small> English writer gives some very good rules for the times and places where smoking may be allowed.

H<small>e</small> says: 'But what shall I say of the fragrant weed which Raleigh taught our gallants to puff in capacious bowls; which a royal pedant denounced in a famous "Counterblast"; which his flattering laureate, Ben Jonson, ridiculed to please his master; which our wives and sisters protest gives rise to the dirtiest and most unsociable habit a man can indulge in; of which some fair favourers declare that they love the smell, and others that they will never marry an indulger (which, by the way, they generally end in doing); which has won a fame over more space and among better men than Noah's grape has ever done; which doctors still dispute about, and boys still get sick over; but which is the solace of the weary labourer; the support of the ill-fed; the refresher of overwrought brains; the soother

of angry fancies; the boast of the exquisite; the excuse
of the idle; the companion of the philosopher; and
the tenth muse of the poet. I will go neither into the
medical nor the moral question about the dreamy,
calming cloud. I will content myself so far with saying
what may be said for everything that can bless and
curse mankind, that, in moderation, it is at least
harmless; but what is moderate and what is not, must
be determined in each individual case, according to
the habits and constitution of the subject. If it cures
asthma, it may destroy digestion; if it soothes the
nerves, it may, in excess, produce a chronic irritability.

'But I will regard it in a social point of view; and,
first, as a narcotic, notice its effects on the individual
character. I believe, then, that in moderation it
diminishes the violence of the passions, and,
particularly, that of the temper. Interested in the
subject, I have taken care to seek instances of members
of the same family having the same violent tempers by
inheritance, of whom the one has been calmed down
by smoking, and the other gone on in his passionate
course. I believe that it induces a habit of calm
reflectiveness, which causes us to take less prejudiced,
perhaps less zealous views of life, and to be, therefore,
less irritable in our converse with our fellow creatures.
I am inclined to think that the clergy, the squirearchy,
and the peasantry are the most prejudiced and most
violent classes in this country; there may be other
reasons for this, but it is noteworthy that these are the
classes which smoke least. On the other hand, I confess
that it induces a certain lassitude, and a lounging, easy
mode of life, which are fatal both to the precision of

manners and the vivacity of conversation. The mind of a smoker is contemplative rather than active; and if the weed cures our irritability, it kills our wit. I believe that it is a fallacy to suppose that it encourages drinking. There is more drinking and less smoking in England than in any other country of the civilised world. There was more drinking among the gentry of last century, who never smoked at all. Smoke and wine do not go well together. Coffee or beer are its best accompaniments, and the one cannot intoxicate, the other must be largely imbibed to do so. I have observed among young bachelors that very little wine is drunk in their chambers, and that beer is gradually taking its place. The cigar, too, is an excuse for rising from the dinner-table where there are no ladies to go to.'

'IN another point of view, I am inclined to think that smoking has conduced to make the society of men, when alone, less riotous, less quarrelsome, and even less vicious than it was. Where young men now blow a common cloud, they were formerly driven to a fearful consumption of wine, and this in their heads, they were ready and roused to any iniquity. But the pipe is the bachelor's wife. With it he can endure solitude longer, and is not forced into low society in order to shun it. With it, too, the idle can pass many an hour, which otherwise he would have given, not to work, but to extravagant devilries. With it he is no longer restless and impatient for excitement of any kind. We never hear now of young blades issuing in bands from their wine to beat the watch or disturb the slumbering citizens, as we did thirty or forty years ago, when smoking was still a rarity; they are all puffing harmlessly in their chambers now. But, on the other hand, I foresee with dread a too tender allegiance to the pipe, to the destruction of good society, and the abandonment of the ladies. No wonder they hate it, dear creatures; the pipe is the worst rival a woman can have, and it is one whose eyes she cannot scratch out; who improves with age, while she herself declines; who has an art which no woman possesses, that of never wearying her devotee; who is silent, yet a companion; costs little, yet gives much pleasure; who, lastly, never upbraids, and always yields the same joy. Ah! this is a powerful rival to wife or maid, and no wonder that at last the woman succumbs, consents, and, rather than lose her lord or master, even supplies the hated herb with her own fair hands.'

———◦◦◦———

'ONE must never smoke, nor even ask to smoke, in the company of the fair. If they know that in a few minutes you will be running off to your cigar, the fair will do well – say it is in a garden, or so – to allow you to bring it out and smoke it there. One must never smoke, again, in the streets; that is, in daylight. The deadly crime may be committed, like burglary, after dark, but not before. One must never smoke in a room inhabited at times by the ladies; thus, a well-bred man who has a wife or sisters, will not offer to smoke in the dining room after dinner. One must never smoke in a public place, where ladies are or might be, for instance, a flower show or promenade. One may smoke in a railway carriage in spite of by-laws, if one has first obtained the consent of everyone present; but if there be a lady there, though she give her consent, smoke not. In nine cases out of ten, she will give it from good nature. One must never smoke in a close carriage; one may ask and obtain leave to smoke when returning from a picnic or expedition in an open carriage. One must never smoke in a theatre, on a race course, nor in church. This last is not, perhaps, a needless caution. In the Belgian churches you see a placard announcing, "Ici on ne mâche pas du tabac." One must never smoke when anybody shows an objection to it. One must never smoke a pipe in the streets; one must never smoke at all in the coffee-room of a hotel. One must never smoke, without consent, in the presence of a clergyman, and one must never offer a cigar to any ecclesiastic.'

'BUT if you smoke, or if you are in the company of smokers, and are to wear your clothes in the presence of ladies afterwards, you must change them to smoke in. A host who asks you to smoke, will generally offer you an old coat for the purpose. You must also, after smoking, rinse the mouth well out, and, if possible, brush the teeth. You should never smoke in another person's house without leave, and you should not ask leave to do so if there are ladies in the house. When you are going to smoke a cigar you should offer one at the same time to anybody present, if not a clergyman or a very old man. You should always smoke a cigar given to you, whether good or bad, and never make any remarks on its quality.'

CHESTERFIELD warns his son against faults in good breeding in the following words, and these warnings will be equally applicable to the student of etiquette in the present day. He says: 'Of the lesser talents, good breeding is the principal and most necessary one, not only as it is very important in itself, but as it adds great lustre to the more solid advantages both of the heart and the mind. I have often touched upon good breeding to you before; so that this letter shall be upon the next necessary qualification to it, which is a genteel and easy manner and carriage, wholly free from those odd tricks, ill-habits, and awkwardnesses, which even many very worthy and sensible people have in their behaviour. However trifling a genteel manner may sound, it is of very great consequence towards pleasing in private life, especially the women, which one time or other, you will think worth pleasing; and I have known many a man from his awkwardness, give people such a dislike of him at first, that all his merit could not get the better of it afterwards. Whereas a genteel manner prepossesses people in your favour, bends them towards you, and makes them wish to be like you.'

'THERE is, likewise, an awkwardness of expression and words, most carefully to be avoided; such as false English, bad pronunciation, old sayings, and common proverbs; which are so many proofs of having kept bad and low company. For example, if, instead of saying that tastes are different, and that every man has his own peculiar one, you should let off a proverb, and say, that "What is one man's meat is another man's poison"; or else, "Everyone as they like, as the good man said when he kissed his cow"; everybody would be persuaded that you had never kept company with anybody above footmen and housemaids.'

'ATTENTION will do all this, and without attention nothing is to be done; want of attention, which is really want of thought, is either folly or madness. You should not only have attention to everything, but a quickness of attention, so as to observe, at once, all the people in the room, their motions, their looks, and their words, and yet without staring at them, and seeming to be an observer. This quick and unobserved observation is of infinite advantage in life, and is to be acquired with care; and, on the contrary, what is called absence, which is thoughtlessness, and want of attention about what is doing, makes a man so like either a fool or a madman, that, for my part, I see no real difference. A fool never has thought; a madman has lost it; and an absent man is, for the time, without it.'

'I WOULD warn you against those disagreeable tricks and awkwardnesses, which many people contract when they are young, by the negligence of their parents, and cannot get quit of them when they are old; such as odd motions, strange postures, and ungenteel carriage. But there is likewise an awkwardness of the mind, that ought to be, and with care may be, avoided; as, for instance, to mistake names; to speak of Mr What-d'ye-call-him, or Mrs Thingum, or How-d'ye-call-her, is excessively awkward and ordinary. To call people by improper titles and appellations is so too. To begin a story or narration when you are not perfect in it, and cannot go through with it, but are forced, possibly, to say, in the middle of it, "I have forgotten the rest," is very unpleasant and bungling. One must be extremely exact, clear, and perspicuous, in everything one says, otherwise, instead of entertaining, or informing others, one only tires and puzzles them.'

NOTHING is in worse taste in society than to repeat the witticisms or remarks of another person as if they were your own. If you are discovered in the larceny of another's ideas, you may originate a thousand brilliant ones afterwards, but you will not gain the credit of one. If you quote your friend's remarks, give them as quotations.

BE cautious in the use of your tongue. Wise men say, that a man may repent when he has spoken, but he will not repent if he keeps silence.

IF you wish to retain a good position in society, be careful to return all the visits which are paid to you, promptly, and do not neglect your calls upon ladies, invalids, and men older than yourself.

IN directing a letter, put first the name of the person for whom it is intended, then the name of the city, then that of the state in which he resides. If you send it to the care of another person, or to a boarding house, or hotel, you can put that name either after the name of your correspondent, or in the left hand corner of the letter – thus: –

Mr J. S. Jones,
Care of Mr T. C. Jones,
Boston,
Mass.

or,

> *Mr J. S. Jones,*
> *Boston,*
> *Mass.*
> *Revere House.*

—◦◦◦—

I F your friend is in the army or navy, put his title before his station after his name, thus: –

> *Capt. L. Lewis, U.S.A.,*

or,

> *Lieutenant T. Roberts, U.S.N.*

—◦◦◦—

I F you send your letter by a private hand, put the name of the bearer in the lower left hand corner of the envelope, but put the name only. 'Politeness of,' – or 'Kindness of,' are obsolete, and not used now at all. Write the direction thus: –

> *J. L. Holmes, Esq.,*
> *Revere House,*
> *Boston,*
> *Mass.*

C. L. Cutts, Esq.

—◦◦◦—

THIS will let your friend, Mr Holmes, know that Mr Cutts is in Boston, which is the object to be gained by putting the name of the bearer on a letter, sent by a private hand.

GUARD AGAINST VULGAR LANGUAGE. There is as much connection between the words and the thoughts as there is between the thoughts and the words; the latter are not only the expression of the former, but they have a power to react upon the soul and leave the stains of their corruption there. A young man who allows himself to use one profane or vulgar word, has not only shown that there is a foul spot on his mind, but by the utterance of that word he extends that spot and inflames it, till, by indulgence, it will soon pollute and ruin the whole soul. Be careful of your words as well as your thoughts. If you can control the tongue, that no improper words are pronounced by it, you will soon be able to control the mind and save it from corruption. You extinguish the fire by smothering it, or by preventing bad thoughts bursting out in language. Never utter a word anywhere, which you would be ashamed to speak in the presence of the most religious man. Try this practice a little, and you will soon have command of yourself.

A CELEBRATED English lawyer gives the following directions for young men entering into business. He says:

'SELECT THE KIND OF BUSINESS THAT SUITS YOUR NATURAL INCLINATIONS AND TEMPERAMENT. – Some men are naturally mechanics; others have a strong aversion to anything like machinery, and so on; one man has a natural taste for one occupation in life, and another for another.'

'I NEVER could succeed as a merchant. I have tried it, unsuccessfully, several times. I never could be content with a fixed salary, for mine is a purely speculative disposition, while others are just the reverse; and therefore all should be careful to select those occupations that suit them best.'

'LET YOUR PLEDGED WORD EVER BE SACRED. – Never promise to do a thing without performing it with the most rigid promptness. Nothing is more valuable to a man in business than the name of always doing as he agrees, and that to the moment. A strict adherence to this rule gives a man the command of half the spare funds within the range of his acquaintance, and encircles him with a host of friends, who may be depended upon in any emergency.'

'WHATEVER YOU DO, DO WITH ALL YOUR MIGHT. – Work at it, if necessary, early and late, in season and out of season, not leaving a stone unturned, and never deferring for a single hour that which can just as well be done *now*. The old proverb is full of truth and meaning

– "Whatever is worth doing at all, is worth doing well." Many a man acquires a fortune by doing his business *thoroughly*, while his neighbour remains poor for life, because he only *half* does his business. Ambition, energy, industry, and perseverance, are indispensable requisites for success in business.'

———❦———

'SOBRIETY. USE NO DESCRIPTION OF INTOXICATING DRINKS. – As no man can succeed in business unless he has a *brain* to enable him to lay his plans, and *reason* to guide him in their execution, so, no matter how bountifully a man may be blessed with intelligence, if his brain is muddled, and his judgement warped by intoxicating drinks, it is impossible for him to carry on business successfully. How many good opportunities have passed never to return, while a man was sipping a "social glass" with a friend! How many a foolish bargain has been made under the influence of the wine-cup, which temporarily makes his victim so *rich*! How many important chances have been put off until tomorrow, and thence forever, because indulgence has thrown the system into a state of lassitude, neutralising the energies so essential to success in business. The use of intoxicating drinks as a beverage is as much an infatuation as is the smoking of opium by the Chinese, and the former is quite as destructive to the success of the business man as the latter.'

———❦———

'LET HOPE PREDOMINATE, BUT BE NOT TOO VISIONARY. – Many persons are always kept poor because they are too *visionary*. Every project looks to them like certain success, and, therefore, they keep changing from one business to another, always in hot water, and always "under the harrow". The plan of "counting the chickens before they are hatched", is an error of ancient date, but it does not seem to improve by age.'

―⁕―

'**D**O NOT SCATTER YOUR POWERS. – Engage in one kind of business only, and stick to it faithfully until you succeed, or until you conclude to abandon it. A constant hammering on one nail will generally drive it home at last, so that it can be clinched. When a man's undivided attention is centred on one object, his mind will continually be suggesting improvements of value, which would escape him if his brain were occupied by a dozen different subjects at once. Many a fortune has slipped through men's fingers by engaging in too many occupations at once.'

―⁕―

'**E**NGAGE PROPER EMPLOYEES. – Never employ a man of bad habits when one whose habits are good can be found to fill his situation. I have generally been extremely fortunate in having faithful and competent persons to fill the responsible situations in my business; and a man can scarcely be too grateful for such a blessing. When you find a man unfit to fill his station, either from incapacity or peculiarity of character or disposition, dispense with his services, and do not drag out a miserable existence in the vain attempt to change his nature. It is utterly impossible to do so, "You cannot make a silk purse," etc. He has been created for some other sphere; let him find and fill it.'

―⁕―

I F you wish to succeed in society, and be known as a man who converses well, you must cultivate your memory. Do not smile and tell me that this is a gift, not an acquirement. It is true that some people have naturally a more retentive memory than others, but those naturally most deficient may strengthen their powers by cultivation.

———

C ULTIVATE, therefore, this glorious faculty, by storing and exercising it with trains of imagery. Accustom yourselves to look at any natural object, and then consider how many facts and thoughts may be associated with it – how much of poetic imagery and refined combinations. Follow out this idea, and you will find that imagination, which is too often in youth permitted to build up castles in the air, tenantless as they are unprofitable, will become, if duly exercised, a source of much enjoyment. I was led into this train of thought while walking in a beautiful country, and seeing before me a glorious rainbow, overarching the valley which lay in front. And not more quickly than its appearance, came to my remembrance an admirable passage in the 'Art of Poetic Painting', wherein the author suggests the great mental advantage of exercising the mind on all subjects, by considering –

What use can be made of them?

What remarks they will illustrate?

What representations they will serve?

What comparison they will furnish?

A ND while thus thinking, I remembered that the ingenious author has instanced the rainbow as affording a variety of illustrations, and capable, in the imagery which it suggests, of numerous combinations. Thus:

THE HUES OF THE RAINBOW

Tinted the green and flowery banks of the stream;
Tinged the white blossoms of the apple orchards;
Shed a beauteous radiance on the grass;
Veiled the waning moon and the evening star;
Overarched the mist of the waterfall;
Reminded the looker-on of peace opposed to turbulence.
And illustrated the moral that even
*   the most beautiful things of earth must pass away.*

E VERY book you read, every natural object which meets your view, may be the exercise of memory, be made to furnish food both for reflection and conversation, enjoyment for your own solitary hours, and the means of making you popular in society. Believe me, the man who – 'saw it, to be sure, but really forgot what it looked like', who is met every day in society, will not be sought after as will the man, who, bringing memory and fancy happily blended to bear upon what he sees, can make every object worthy of remark familiar and interesting to those who have not seen it.

I F you have leisure moments, and what man has not? do not consider them as spare atoms of time to be wasted, idled away in profitless lounging. Always have a book within your reach, which you may catch up at your odd minutes. Resolve to edge in a little reading every day, if it is but a single sentence. If you can give fifteen minutes a day, it will be felt at the end of the year. Thoughts take up no room. When they are right they afford a portable pleasure, which one may travel or labour with without any trouble or encumbrance.

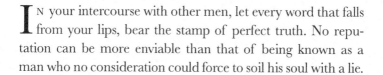

I N your intercourse with other men, let every word that falls from your lips, bear the stamp of perfect truth. No reputation can be more enviable than that of being known as a man who no consideration could force to soil his soul with a lie.

'T RUTH is naturally so acceptable to man, so charming in herself, that to make falsehood be received, we are compelled to dress it up in the snow-white robes of Truth; as in passing base coin, it must have the impress of the good ere it will pass current. Deception, hypocrisy, and dissimulation, are, when practised, direct compliments to the power of Truth; and the common custom of passing off Truth's counterfeit for herself, is strong testimony in behalf of her intrinsic beauty and excellence.'

N EXT to being a man of talent, a well-read man is the most agreeable in society, and no investment of money or time is so profitable as that spent in good, useful books, and reading. A good book is a lasting companion. Truths, which it has taken years to glean, are therein at once freely but carefully communicated. We enjoy communion with the mind, though not with the person of the writer. Thus the humblest man may surround himself by the wisest and best spirits of past and present ages. No one can be solitary who possesses a book; he owns a friend that will instruct him in moments of leisure or of necessity. It is only necessary to turn open the leaves, and the fountain at once gives forth its streams. You may seek costly furniture for your homes, fanciful ornaments for your mantel-pieces, and rich carpets for your floors; but, after the absolute necessaries for a home, give me books as at once the cheapest, and certainly the most useful and abiding embellishments.

A TRUE gentleman will not only refrain from ridiculing the follies, ignorance, or infirmities of others, but he will not even allow himself to smile at them. He will treat the rudest clown with the same easy courtesy which he would extend to the most polished gentleman, and will never by word, look, or gesture show that he notices the faults, or vulgarity of another. *Personal deformity* is a cross sent by God, and none but a depraved, wicked, and brutal man could ridicule, or even greet with a passing smile the unfortunate thus stamped. Even a word or look of pity will wound the sensitive, but frank, gentle courtesy, the regard paid by a feeling man to the comfort of a cripple, or that easy grace which, while it shows no sign of seeing the deformity, shows more deference to the afflicted one than to the more fortunate, are all duly appreciated and acknowledged, and win for the man who extends them the respect and love of all with whom he comes in contact.

REMEMBER that true wit never descends to person-alities. When you hear a man trying to be 'funny' at the expense of his friends, or even his enemies, you may feel sure that his *humour* is forced, and while it sinks to ill nature, cannot rise to the level of true *wit*.

NEVER try to make yourself out to be a very important person. If you are so really, your friends will soon find it out, if not, they will not give you credit for being so, because you try to force your fancied importance upon them. A pompous fool, though often seen, is not much loved nor respected, and you may remember that the frog who tried to make himself as big as an ox, died in the attempt.

A SEVERE wit once said, 'If you do not wish to be the mark for slanderous tongues, be the first to enter a room, and the last to leave it.'

IF you are ever tempted to speak against a woman, think first – 'Suppose she were my sister!' You can never gain anything by bringing your voice against a woman, even though she may deserve contempt, and your forbearance may shame others into a similar silence. It is a cowardly tongue that will take a woman's name upon it to injure her; though many men do this, who would fear, – *absolutely be afraid*, to speak against a man, or that same woman, had she a manly arm to protect her.

I AGAIN quote from the celebrated Lord Chesterfield, who says: 'It is good-breeding alone that can prepossess people in your favour at first sight, more time being necessary to discover greater talents. This good breeding, you know, does not consist in low bows and formal ceremony; but in an easy, civil, and respectful behaviour. You will take care, therefore, to answer with complaisance, when you are spoken to; to place yourself at the lower end of the table, unless bid to go higher; to drink first to the lady of the house, and next to the master; not to eat awkwardly or dirtily; not to sit when others stand; and to do all this with an air of complaisance, and not with a grave, sour look, as if you did it all unwillingly. I do not mean a silly, insipid smile, that fools have when they would be civil; but an air of sensible good-humour.'

'I MENTIONED the general rules of common civility, which, whoever does not observe, will pass for a bear, and be as unwelcome as one, in company; there is hardly anybody brutal enough not to answer when they are spoken to. But it is not enough not to be rude; you should be extremely civil, and distinguished for your good breeding. The first principle of this good breeding is never to say anything that you think can be disagreeable to anybody in company; but, on the contrary, you should endeavour to say what will be agreeable to them; and that in an easy and natural manner, without seeming to study for compliments. There is likewise such a thing as a civil look, and a rude look; and you should look civil, as well as be so; for if, while you are saying a civil thing, you look gruff and surly, as English bumpkins do, nobody will be obliged to you for a civility that seemed to come so unwillingly.'

———⦿———

'CIVILITY is particularly due to all women; and remember, that no provocation whatsoever can justify any man in not being civil to every woman; and the greatest man would justly be reckoned a brute, if he were not civil to the meanest woman. It is due to their sex, and is the only protection they have against the superior strength of ours; nay, even a little flattery is allowable with women; and a man may, without meanness, tell a woman that she is either handsomer or wiser than she is. Observe the French people, and mind how easily and naturally civil their address is, and how agreeably they insinuate little civilities in their conversation. They think it so essential, that they call an honest man and a civil man by the same name, of *honnête homme*; and the Romans called civility *humanitas*, as thinking it inseparable from humanity. You cannot begin too early to take that turn, in order to make it natural and habitual to you.'

———⦿———

FLATTERY is always in bad taste. If you say more in a person's praise than is deserved, you not only say what is *false*, but you make others doubt the wisdom of your judgement. Open, palpable flattery will be regarded by those to whom it is addressed as an insult. In your intercourse with ladies, you will find that the delicate compliment of seeking their society, showing your pleasure in it, and choosing for subjects of conversation, other themes than the weather, dress, or the opera, will be more appreciated by women of sense, than the more awkward compliment of open words or gestures of admiration.

NEVER imitate the eccentricities of other men, even though those men have the highest genius to excuse their oddities. Eccentricity is, at the best, in bad taste; but an imitation of it – second hand oddity – is detestable.

IN giving an entertainment to your friends, while you avoid extravagant expenditure, it is your duty to place before them the best your purse will permit you to purchase, and be sure you have plenty. Abundance without superfluity, and good quality without extravagance, are your best rules for an entertainment.

IF, by the introduction of a friend, by a mistake, or in any other way, your enemy, or a man to whom you have the strongest personal dislike, is under your roof, or at your table, as a guest, hospitality and good breeding both require you to treat him with the same frank courtesy which you extend to your other guests; though you need make no violent prot-estations of friendship, and are not required to make any advances towards him after he ceases to be your guest.

I N giving a dinner party, invite only as many guests as you can seat comfortably at your table. If you have two tables, have them precisely alike, or, rest assured, you will offend those friends whom you place at what they judge to be the inferior table. Above all, avoid having little tables placed in the corners of the room, when there is a large table. At some houses in Paris it is a fashion to set the dining room entirely with small tables, which will accommodate comfortably three or four people, and such parties are very merry, very sociable and pleasant, if four congenial people are around each table; but it is a very dull fashion, if you are not sure of the congeniality of each quartet of guests.

I F you lose your fortune or position in society, it is wiser to retire from the world of fashion than to wait for that world to bow you out.

I F you are poor, but welcome in society on account of your family or talents, avoid the error which the young are most apt to fall into, that of living beyond your means.

T HE advice of Polonius to Laertes is as excellent in the present day, as it was in Shakespeare's time:

Give thy thoughts no tongue,
Nor any unproportioned thought his act.

Be thou familiar, but by no means vulgar.
The friends thou hast, and their adoption tried,
Grapple them to thy soul with hooks of steel:
But do not dull thy palm with entertainments
Of each new hatch'd, unfledg'd comrade.
Beware of entrance to a quarrel: but, being in,
Bear it that the opposer may beware of thee.
Give every man thine ear, but few thy voice;
Take each man's censure, but reserve thy judgement.
Costly thy habit as thy purse can buy,
But not express'd in fancy; rich, not gaudy;
For the apparel oft proclaims the man.

IT is by no means desirable to be always engaged in the serious pursuits of life. Take time for pleasure, and you will find your work progresses faster for some recreation. Lord Chesterfield says: 'I do not regret the time that I passed in pleasures; they were seasonable; they were the pleasures of youth, and I enjoyed them while young. If I had not, I should probably have overvalued them now, as we are very apt to do what we do not know; but knowing them as I do, I know their real value, and how much they are generally overrated. Nor do I regret the time that I have passed in business, for the same reason; those who see only the outside of it, imagine it has hidden charms, which they pant after; and nothing but acquaintance can undeceive them. I, who have been behind the scenes, both of pleasure and business, and have seen all the springs and pulleys of those decorations which astonish and dazzle the audience, retire, not only without regret, but with contentment and satisfaction.'

THE same author, speaking of the evils of pedantry, says: – 'Every excellency, and every virtue has its kindred vice or weakness; and, if carried beyond certain bounds, sinks into one or the other. Generosity often runs into profusion, economy into avarice, courage into rashness, caution into timidity, and so on – insomuch that, I believe, there is more judgement required for the proper conduct of our virtues, than for avoiding their opposite vices. Vice, in its true light, is so deformed, that it shocks us at first sight, and would hardly ever seduce us, if it did not at first wear the mask of some virtue. But virtue is, in itself, so beautiful, that it charms us at first sight; engages us more and more upon further acquaintance; and, as with other beauties, we think excess impossible, it is here that judgement is necessary, to moderate and direct the effects of an excellent cause.'

SOME learned men, proud of their knowledge, only speak to decide, and give judgement without appeal; the consequence of which is, that mankind, provoked by the insult, and injured by the oppression, revolt; and, in order to shake off the tyranny, even call the lawful authority in question. The more you know, the modester you should be; and (by the by) that modesty is the surest way of gratifying your vanity. Even where you are sure, seem rather doubtful; represent, but do not pronounce; and, if you would convince others, seem open to conviction yourself.'

'OTHERS, to show their learning, or often from the prejudices of a school education, where they hear of nothing else, are always talking of the ancients, as something more than men, and of the moderns, as something less. They are never without a classic or two in their pockets; they stick to the old good sense; they read none of the modern trash; and will show you plainly that no improvement has been made in any one art or science these last seventeen hundred years. I would, by no means, have you disown your acquaintance with the ancients; but still less would I have you brag of an exclusive intimacy with them. Speak of the moderns without contempt, and of the ancients without idolatry; judge them all by their merits, but not by their ages; and if you happen to have an Elzevir classic in your pocket, neither show it nor mention it.'

'SOME great scholars, most absurdly, draw all their maxims, both for public and private life, from what they call parallel cases in the ancient authors; without considering that, in the first place, there never were, since the creation of the world, two cases exactly parallel; and, in the next place, that there never was a case stated, or even known, by any historian, with every one of its circumstances; which, however, ought to be known in order to be reasoned from. Reason upon the case itself, and the several circumstances that attend it, and act accordingly; but not from the authority of ancient poets or historians. Take into your consideration, if you please, cases seemingly analogous; but take them as helps only, not as guides.'

I F you are poor, you must deprive yourself often of the pleasure of escorting ladies to ride, the opera, or other entertainments, because it is understood in society that, in these cases, a gentleman pays all the expenses for both, and in any emergency you may find your bill for carriage hire, suppers, bouquets, or other unforeseen demands, greater than you anticipated.

S HUN the card table. Even the friendly games common in society, for small stakes, are best avoided. They feed the love of gambling, and you will find that this love, if once acquired, is the hardest curse to get rid of.

I T is in bad taste, though often done, to turn over the cards on a table, when you are calling. If your host or hostess finds you so doing, it may lead them to suppose you value them more for their acquaintances than themselves.

HESPERUS PRESS • 28 Mortimer Street, London, W1W 7RD
• T: 0207 436 0869 • www.hesperuspress.com

HESPERUS